Culture and Customs of Morocco

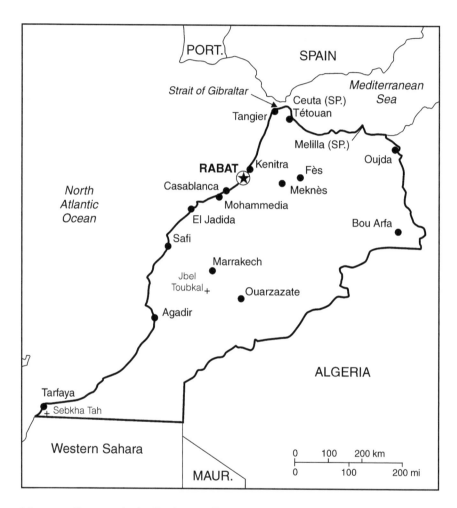

Morocco. Cartography by Bookcomp, Inc.

Culture and Customs
of Morocco

∽∘∾

RAPHAEL CHIJIOKE NJOKU

Culture and Customs of Africa
Toyin Falola, Series Editor

GREENWOOD PRESS
Westport, Connecticut • London

Library of Congress Cataloging-in-Publication Data

Njoku, Raphael Chijioke.
   Culture and customs of Morocco / by Raphael Chijioke Njoku.
      p. cm. — (Culture and customs of Africa, ISSN 1530–8367)
   Includes bibliographical references and index.
   ISBN 0–313–33289–4
   1. Morocco—Civilization. 2. Morocco—Social life and customs.
I. Title. II. Series.
DT312.N57 2006
964—dc22   2005026178

British Library Cataloguing in Publication Data is available.

Library of Congress Catalog Card Number: 2005026178
ISBN: 0–313–33289–4
ISSN: 1530–8367

First published in 2006

Greenwood Press, 88 Post Road West, Westport, CT 06881
An imprint of Greenwood Publishing Group, Inc.
www.greenwood.com

Printed in the United States of America

The paper used in this book complies with the
Permanent Paper Standard issued by the National
Information Standards Organization (Z39.48–1984).

10 9 8 7 6 5 4 3 2 1

For my daughter Chinma Emmanuelle Njoku

Contents

Series Foreword

AFRICA is a vast continent, the second largest, after Asia. It is four times the size of the United States, excluding Alaska. It is the cradle of human civilization. A diverse continent, Africa has more than 50 countries with a population of over 700 million people who speak over 1,000 languages. Ecological and cultural differences vary from one region to another. As an old continent, Africa is one of the richest in culture and customs, and its contributions to world civilization are impressive indeed.

Africans regard culture as essential to their lives and future development. Culture embodies their philosophy, worldview, behavior patterns, arts, and institutions. The books in this series intend to capture the comprehensiveness of African culture and customs, dwelling on such important aspects as religion, worldview, literature, media, art, housing, architecture, cuisine, traditional dress, gender, marriage, family, lifestyles, social customs, music, and dance.

The uses and definitions of "culture" vary, reflecting its prestigious association with civilization and social status, its restriction to attitude and behavior in globalization, and the debates surrounding issues of tradition, modernity, and postmodernity. The participating authors have chosen a comprehensive meaning of culture while not ignoring the alternative uses of the term. Each volume in the series focuses on a single country, and the format is uniform. The first chapter presents a historical overview, in addition to information on geography, economy, and politics. Each volume then proceeds to examine the various aspects of culture and customs. The series highlights the mechanisms for the transmission of tradition and culture across generations: the significance of orality, traditions, kinship rites, and family property distribution; the rise of print culture; and the impact of educational institutions. The series also explores the intersection between local, regional, national, and global bases for identity and social relations. While the volumes are organized nationally, they pay attention to ethnicity and language groups and the links between Africa and the wider world.

The books in the series capture the elements of continuity and change in culture and customs. Custom is not represented as static or as a museum artifact, but as a dynamic phenomenon. Furthermore, the authors recognize the current challenges to traditional wisdom, which include gender relations; the negotiation of local identities in relation to the state; the significance of struggles for power at national and local levels and their impact on cultural traditions and community-based forms of authority; and the tensions between agrarian and industrial/manufacturing/ oil-based economic modes of production.

Africa is a continent of great changes, instigated mainly by Africans but also through influences from other continents. The rise of youth culture, the penetration of the global media, and the challenges to generational stability are some of the components of modern changes explored in the series. The ways in which traditional (non-Western and nonimitative) African cultural forms continue to survive and thrive, that is, how they have taken advantage of the market system to enhance their influence and reproductions also receive attention.

Through the books in this series, readers can see their own cultures in a different perspective, understand the habits of Africans, and educate themselves about the customs and cultures of other countries and people. The hope is that the readers will come to respect the cultures of others and see them not as inferior or superior to theirs, but merely as different. Africa has always been important to Europe and the United States, essentially as a source of labor, raw materials, and markets. Blacks are in Europe and the Americas as part of the African diaspora, a migration that took place primarily due to the slave trade. Recent African migrants increasingly swell their number and visibility. It is important to understand the history of the diaspora and the newer migrants, as well as the roots of the culture and customs of the places from where they come. It is equally important to understand others in order to be able to interact successfully in a world that keeps shrinking. The accessible nature of the books in this series will contribute to this understanding and enhance the quality of human interaction in a new millennium.

Toyin Falola
Frances Higginbotham, Nalle Centennial Professor in History
The University of Texas at Austin

Preface

MOROCCO is a strategically located North African country. Historically, it has been a melting pot of different civilizations, including African, European, Middle Eastern, and Asian cultures. This accounts for the country's rich and elaborate traditional practices and customs. This book explores Moroccan ways of life with a particular focus on aspects that distinctly define the uniqueness of the country and its people, its society and institutions, and the lifestyle of a new generation of people gradually turning away from the strict religious observances of the older generations.

Notwithstanding the pervading Pan-Islamic identity in practice, certain elements of Berber indigenous traditions and customs have proved resilient. Long before the beginning of the twentieth-century European imperialism in Africa, the indigenous Berbers of North Africa had made contact with different imperial powers and visitors, exchanging goods, curiosities, gifts, religion, political systems, and ideas with the Phoenicians, Romans, Vandals, Arabs, and so on. French colonialism introduced Western-style bureaucracy, education, technology, cash economy, and new cities, developmental infrastructures and modern amenities that have reordered preexisting institutions and the people's lifestyles. This book provides a sense of social change in a historical context. It introduces the reader to the making of a hybrid socioeconomic milieu within which Arab, European, and African cultural traditions combined with indigenous practices in fashioning ideas, values, norms, and manners that one can today regard as Moroccan.

Acknowledgments

THE SAYING THAT NO one person has written a book is most applicable to the circumstances that have seen me through this project. First, I benefited immensely from the expertise of my editor, Ms. Wendi Schnaufer. Her immense experience was mostly demonstrated in her patience and brilliant suggestions for improved standards and general conformity with style and content.

I owe special thanks to Professor Toyin Falola, who invited me to write the book, discussed the project with me at the initial stage, and encouraged me to produce a good work. His continued communication and very generous contributions served as a reminder that I should keep up progress on the project.

With normal teaching and other professional engagements serving as a serious distraction, I relied heavily on the help provided by my research assistants and other colleagues in Morocco, Belgium, and the United States. Nasr Yahyaoui, Habib Essbai, Abdenasser Essbai, Lekan and Abimbola Badru, Elizabeth Smith, Melinda Nicole Daniel, Denise Martin, and Susanne Dickmann read different drafts of this manuscript and provided immense input. Then came help from colleagues and friends Professors Lateef O. Badru, John Mackey, John McLeod, Bruce Adams, Benjamin Harrison, Karen Spierling, Scott Levi, Mary Bani, Ricky Jones, Blaine Hudson, Theresa Rajack-Tallyey, and Rita Hettinger.

I owe immense gratitude to Professor Valérie K. Orlando of Illinois Wesleyan University in Bloomington for her generosity with time and resources. Ms. Lee Keeling, ever helpful, handled the formatting of the manuscript and pictures according to acceptable standards.

Finally but not the least, I must not forget to thank my undergraduate and graduate students of 2004 who discussed the idea of this project and conducted research on a number of topics. Their contributions and support are highly appreciated.

Part of the funds for this research was provided by the Dean's Incentive Fund and by the African American Development Fund of the School of Arts and Social Sciences (University of Louisville, Kentucky).

Chronology

40,000–25,000 B.C.E.	Indication of an advanced Paleolithic culture or cave dwellers in the entire Mediterranean region.
3000–2200 B.C.E.	Ancient Egyptian, Greek, and Roman sources record presence of the Berber people of North Africa in the area known today as Morocco.
2000 B.C.E.	Sahara region begins to desiccate.
1200 B.C.E.	Phoenicians, a seafaring people, arrive in North Africa. Although they mainly settle in Tunis, their presence is also significant in the Moroccan towns of Tangier and Chellah (near Tétouan).
c. 146 B.C.E.	Beginning of Carthaginian influence in Morocco, lasting until the arrival of the Romans.
429 C.E.	Vandals defeat the Roman imperial power and by extension assumed control of North Africa.
683	Arab people of the Arabian Peninsula invade North Africa.
710	End of Berber resistance to Arab presence and the beginning of their conversion to the Islamic religion.

785–790	Arrival of Moulay Idriss I and the establishment of the foremost Muslim dynasty, know as the Idrissid (descendants of the Prophet Muhammad). The Idrisses rule Morocco for about 200 years (789–987 C.E.).
807–808	City of Fez founded by the Idriss rulers.
818	Arabs are expelled from Spanish lands, and hundreds of Arab families arrive in Morocco from Cordoba.
c. 1000–1700	Succession of dynasties and religious movements, including the Almoravid (c. 1061–1148) and Almohad dynasties (c. 1148–1269), which at their respective peaks control all of Morocco and parts of present-day Algeria and Spain.
1070	City of Marrakech, located in the midwestern region of Morocco, is established by the Almohad rulers.
1666–1672	Alawis, or Alouites, the current ruling dynasty, establishes its monarchical authority under Moulay Ismail.
1860	Quarrel over Spain's Ceuta enclave; Spain declares war and wins a further enclave and an enlarged Ceuta in the settlement.
1884	Spain claims a protectorate in coastal areas of Morocco.
1904	France and Spain agree on their respective zones of influence in Morocco.
1906	Algerian (in French, Algeciras) Conference in Spain; France and Spain get the go-ahead to police Moroccan ports and collect customs fees.
1912, March 30	Morocco becomes a French protectorate under the Treaty of Fez, administered by French Resident-General Louis Hubert Gonzalve Lyautey (1854–1934), although Berber resistance continues until 1933. Spain continues to operate its coastal protectorate. The sultan of Morocco maintains a largely figurehead role.

1927, November 18	Mohammed Ibn Youssef (1911–1961; later Mohammed V) succeeds his father as the Sultan of Morocco at the age of 18.
1929, July 9	Birth of Hassan (1929–1999) in Rabat, who later reigns as King Hassan II.
1933	Remnants of Berber resistance to French colonial control are pacified. The colonialists set up an indirect rule system in the region.
1943	Istiqlal (Independence) Party is established to press for an end to colonial rule.
1947, April 9	Sultan Youssef's historic trip to the northern city of Tangier, during which his bold nationalist speech revives the nationalist consciousness and resistance to French colonial rule in Morocco.
1953, August 20	Sultan Youssef and family are exiled to Madagascar by French Resident-General Theodore Steege.
1955, November 16	Sultan Mohammed Youssef and the royal family return from exile.
1956, March 2	Madrid Accord establishes the end of the French protectorate. Spain keeps its two coastal enclaves of Ceuta and Melilla.
1956, March 3	Sultan Mohammed Ibn Youssef declares himself King Mohammed V.
1961, February	Death of King Mohammed V; King Hassan II succeeds his father.
1963	Historic general parliamentary elections held in Morocco.
1963, August 21	Birth of Crown Prince Sidi Mohammed.
1965	Amid growing social unrest, King Hassan II declares a state of emergency and suspends parliament.
1971	Attempted military coup fails to depose the king and establish a republic.
1973	Polisario movement begins. It aims to establish an independent state in Spanish Sahara, a territory

south of Morocco. Algeria declares support for the movement.

1975, November 6	Green March Day: King Hassan II orders 350,000 civilian volunteers to cross into Western Sahara in a dramatic show of solidarity for the king in his claim over the territory for the state of Morocco.
1975, December	Spain signs the Madrid Accords, withdrawing from Spanish Sahara (soon to become Western Sahara) and transferring it to joint Moroccan-Mauritanian control. Amid objections and threats of military intervention from Algeria, Moroccan forces enter and occupy the territory.
1976, February	Moroccan and Algerian troops clash in Western Sahara. Algeria announces the formation of the Saharawi Arab Democratic Republic (SADR) and forms a government in exile. Morocco and Mauritania divide Western Sahara.
1976	Fighting between the Moroccan military and Polisario (nationalist forces) over the sovereignty of Western Sahara.
1983	Meeting between King Hassan II and the Algerian president aims to achieve better relations between the two neighbors.
1983	King Hassan II cancels planned elections amid political unrest and economic crisis.
1984	Morocco leaves the Organization of African Unity in protest at the admission of the Saharawi Arab Democratic Republic (SADR) to the continental body. Polisario claims to have killed more than 5,000 Moroccan soldiers in offensives between 1982 and 1985.
1988	Morocco resumes full diplomatic relations with Algeria.
1991	United Nations–monitored ceasefire begins in Western Sahara, but the territory's status remains

	undecided and numerous ceasefire violations are reported.
1998	First opposition leader, Abderrahmare Youssoufi, becomes official.
1999, July 23	Death of King Hassan II; his son, Sidi, takes over as Mohammed VI.
2001, November	King Mohammed VI starts a controversial tour of Western Sahara, the first by a Moroccan monarch in a decade.
2002, July	Morocco and Spain agree to a U.S.-brokered resolution over the disputed island of Perejil. Spanish troops had taken the island after noticing the unusual presence of Moroccan soldiers.
2002, December	Morocco and Spain unsuccessfully try to reestablish full diplomatic relations after the conflict over the disputed island of Perejil in July.
2003, February	Casablanca court jails three Saudi members of al-Qaeda for 10 years after they are accused of plotting to attack U.S. and British warships in the Strait of Gibraltar in 2002.
2003, May 7	Forty-one people are killed and many are injured in a series of suicide bomb attacks in Casablanca, allegedly funded by al-Qaeda.
2004, February	Morocco is hit by strong earthquake, leaving more than 600 people dead. The quake shakes rural areas near the Mediterranean city of Al Hoceima, affecting primarily three remote villages—Ait Kamra, Tamassint, and Imzourn.
2004, August 24, 29	Hicham El Guerrouj, one of Morocco's most accomplished athletes, wins the 1,500 and 5,000 meters titles at the 2004 Olympic Games in Athens, Greece.
2004, October 9	Mohammed VI appoints Driss Jettou as prime minister and leader of government business.

2005, August 18   Polisario Front releases 404 Moroccan POWs held since the UN-brokered ceasefire in 1991.

2005, August 20   His Majesty King Mohammed VI orders the release of 417 prisoners, including political prisoners, on the occasion of the 52nd anniversary of the Revolution of the King and People.

1

Introduction

Morocco is like a tree, whose roots lie in Africa,
but whose leaves breathe in European air.
*(Le Maroc est comme un arbre, dont les racines se situent
en Afrique, mais dont les feuilles en air européen.)*
—King Hassan II of Morocco (ruled 1961–1999)

THE KINGDOM OF MOROCCO is the most westerly of the North African states. It is one of the key African countries of the Maghreb (Arabic for "further west") region that includes Morocco, Algeria, and Tunisia. Its area of 174,000 square miles (446,550 square kilometers), including plains, mountains, and stretches of desert wasteland, is just slightly larger than the state of California in the United States. Morocco, sometimes called Al mamlaka al Maghribia, has an estimated population of more than 32 million, which continues to grow at an annual rate of 1.61 percent, with a birthrate as high as 22.79 births per 1,000 and a mortality rate of 5.71 deaths per 1,000 population. The average life expectancy at birth for the total population is approximately 70.35 years (male, 68.06 years; female, 72.74 years). The capital is the north-eastern coastal city of Rabat; however, the largest and most famous is the chief port city of Casablanca. Cultural ideas and institutions are as varied as geographical conditions.

As depicted in the 1942 film *Casablanca,* starring Humphrey Bogart, Morocco typically appears in the minds of many foreigners as a mysteri-ously different land. It remained independent for centuries as it developed a rich culture blended from Berber, Arab, African, and European influences.

Morocco eventually became a French colony in 1912 while the Spanish controlled the small port cities of Ceuta and Melilla in the north and the Spanish Sahara in the south. After 44 years of Franco-Spanish colonialism, the country regained its independence on March 2, 1956, with Sultan Mohammed V, also known as Mohammed ben Youssef (ruled 1927–1961) as the head of government. Postcolonial Morocco is yet to establish a full-fledged democracy. King Mohammed V died in 1961 and was succeeded by his son, Hassan II, who ruled for 38 years. Under Hassan II (ruled 1961–1999), the emergent nationalist political parties maintained a nominal presence and his piecemeal political reforms in the 1990s resulted in the establishment of a bicameral legislature in 1997. Given the sizable number of its indigenous Jews, Morocco under Hassan was favorably disposed toward a vital Arab peace with the state of Israel. At his father King Hassan II's death in 1999, Mohammed VI succeeded to the throne. Although human rights groups criticized the late king for his brutal response to political opponents, his successor was widely perceived as a leader who would press on with democratic openings. Parliamentary elections were held in September 2002, the second time since August 1970 when the late King Hassan first endorsed a new constitution and restored parliamentary government. Municipal elections followed in September 2003. Morocco, with strong support from Spain, is angling for membership in the European Union (EU), its principal trading partner. So far, there appears to be little enthusiasm for the idea among the EU leaders—probably because of some intractable problems plaguing the North African country.

Morocco is faced with a number of issues that need be addressed to win a more favorable international acceptance. To the south, the issue of its annexation of Western Sahara in the late 1970s remains unresolved, pending the outcome of a proposed referendum on self-determination that Morocco has so far not allowed. To the north, a dispute with Spain in July 2002 over the small island of Perejil revived the issue of the sovereignty of the Spanish-controlled islands of Ceuta and Melilla, on the Mediterranean coast. More recently, the involvement of its citizens in the Madrid (Spain) terrorist train bombing in March 2004 has hindered any advance in Morocco's international relations.

Religious fundamentalism and terrorist activities are heavily funded with profits from illicit drug trafficking in cannabis, hashish, and marijuana. Morocco is the world's largest exporter of cannabis, cultivated in the rugged countryside of the Rif Mountains, especially in the districts of Ghafsai and Taounat. Until the recent wave of terrorist bombings in the country, the Moroccan government has not done much to fight against the powerful cartel that runs the over 8 billion dollar drug trade in Morocco. While addicts openly have their fix, European visitors and smugglers have also found it easy to traffic drugs and sex with young boys in the streets. With pressures from the United Nations Office on Drugs and Crime (UNODC), the United States, and other Western governments, the authorities in Morocco have recently launched a more aggressive campaign against these illicit businesses. In 2004, for instance, a total of 687 foreign smugglers were apprehended. Unless the government is able to resolve these and other issues, it is unlikely that Morocco will realize its dreams of a closer and more respectable relationship with the Western world.

LAND

Morocco is strategically placed at the geographical intersection between Europe, Asia, and the rest of Africa. It borders the Atlantic Ocean to the west; to the north are the Mediterranean Sea, the Straight of Gibraltar, and Spain; to the south are Western Sahara and the Sahara, and to the east is Algeria. The country's geography is diverse and divided into five regions by a stretch of rugged mountainous landscapes. The Rif Mountains parallel the Mediterranean coast from Ceuta to Melilla, with large areas of flanking plateau, valleys, and rich coastal plains. The coastal plains of western Morocco stretch from the northern city of Tangier southward to Essaouira, where the High Atlas Mountains interrupt the plains that reach the sea at that point. The mountains are divided into three areas, the Middle Atlas, the High Atlas, and the Anti-Atlas ranges. To the south of the Rif and the Sebou (or Sebu) River basin is the Middle Atlas, separated from the eastern fringes of the High Atlas farther south by the valley of the Abid River. The High Atlas extend some 450 miles in length and forty miles in width and divide the country into two distinct climatic zones—one that receives the westerly winds from the Atlantic and one that is influenced by the proximity of the Sahara. The Anti-Atlas to the south, the homeland of the Amazigh Berbers, is connected with the High Atlas by means of the volcanic massif of Siroua. Farther to the south of the Anti-Atlas are oases *(smara),* seasonal rivers, and little island towns. This complex network of mountains, plateaus, valleys, rivers, seas, and oceans brings about climatic diversities that are difficult to summarize.

In broad terms, the north is considered warm and temperate and the south semiarid. The Mediterranean climate in the western and northern Morocco is strongly modified by local factors such as the mountain ranges and proximity to the seas. The Rif and the Atlas chains act as a barrier between western and eastern parts of the country. The westerly winds that come off the Atlantic in the winter bring snow and rain to the western flanks of the mountains, leaving little to the eastern steppes and plains. The temperature does not fall below

46 degrees except in the Middle Atlas ranges, where the temperature may reach zero degrees and the weather may be harsh. Winter weather conditions may vary from severely cold and rainy to inadequate rainfall, which is usually accompanied by poor agricultural production.

Rainfall in spring is usually slight and irregular, and the mean temperature is about 68 degrees. Around the Mediterranean coast, the climate is generally mild and sunny. The land around the Atlantic coast has enough rainfall to sustain land fertility and good agricultural yield. Heavy rainfalls occur in some parts of the Rif Mountains, the Middle Atlas ranges, and some areas of Tangier closer to the Strait of Gibraltar, but most parts of the Sahara in the south experiences an average rainfall of less than 4 inches per year.

Summer is generally hot and dry, except along the Mediterranean coast, where it is humid, and in the Rif and Atlas ranges, where the temperatures are cool, although the sun may be fierce. Summer rain occurs only in the mountains and is accompanied by violent storms in June and July—similar to weather often experienced in Appalachia of the United States between June and August. Although it is somewhat cool during winter, the Moroccan desert is unbearably hot in summer. This is largely because of the anticyclone from the North Atlantic close to Portugal, the winds from the northeast *(levante),* and the occasional desert winds, such as the sirocco and *chergui.* The driest months are between April and October. The climate, of course, influences the overall culture of the inhabitants—their agricultural production, settlement patterns, and so on.

About 20.12 percent of Morocco's landmass is agriculturally rich. This includes some fertile lowlands along the coast, which are blessed with the constant flow of rivers. The lands lying between the Atlas and Rif ranges and in the valleys of the Atlas are also very fertile. Alluvial plains are rare but are found around the Rharb Plain and the Sous River Valley. Moving away from the coastal plains, agricultural fertility diminishes as the land rises and moves into the steppe and the mountainous interior. The Atlas Mountains divide the country and the northern fringes of the Sahara in the south. In the south and southeast, the land is poor, with rocks and desert encroachments, and is sparsely inhabited by nomads. As a study on the geography of Morocco notes, the agriculturally rich areas of Morocco—the coastal plains and plateaus and the north and west of the Atlas ranges—are known as inner Morocco, or what the French and Spanish colonial powers in Morocco used to call "useful Morocco" (or *le Maroc utile*).[1]

Inner Morocco, also know as "land of the Makhzen" (or *bled el-Makhzen*), harbors all the big cities and most of the country's population. The descendants of the Arabs that arrived in the seventh century have maintained domicile in and around the arable plains and coastal lowlands. In much of these areas, the population density exceeds 100 persons per square mile. In the highly urbanized, intensively farmed coastal strip centering on Casablanca, the population density reaches more than 1,000 per square mile. In sharp contrast, the population is sparse south of the High Atlas, which run deep into the Sahara. In these areas, the population is concentrated in oases lining the Draa River Valley. In the hills, steppes, and mountains, the local Berbers, who have lived in the area since the time of the Phoenicians, and some Bedouins scratch out a living as herders or traders. The land route to inner Morocco, running from Rabat through Meknès and Fès then northeastward to Taza and to Oujda, is located between the Middle Atlas and the Rif Massif. This is the east–west access route to the coastal cities of Casablanca and Rabat. Together with the Upper Moulouya Valley and the Eastern High Plateau, the highway running through Taza is also one of the three features that geographically divide eastern Morocco.

PEOPLES

Morocco, like most Arab and African societies, contains hundreds of small linguistic communities. In the past, most of these subnationalities were independent and self-sufficient. Today, ethnic boundaries are becoming less salient with centuries of miscegenation and the predominance of Arabic as the language of power and identity. Thus, Berber or Arab identity has become more of a reflection of personal behavior rather than of membership in a distinct and delimited social entity. Morocco's Arab-Berbers constitute a 99.1 percent majority of the population. Its indigenous Jewish elements make up 0.2 percent of the population. Other minorities, including Moors (or Arabs of mixed parentage), black Africans (or Negroes), and Europeans (white immigrants)—who mostly reside in the cities—make up about 0.7 percent of the population.[2] The population's statistics present an interesting combination of youth and ethnic solidarity. About 40 percent of the people are younger than 15 years old, and they mostly live along the Atlantic coast or in the High Atlas Mountains. Like most nations, the people are divided into rural and urban dwellers.

About one-third of Morocco's 32 million people are urban dwellers, and nearly one-third of this number live in Casablanca alone. Segments of the urban population are composed of educated Moroccans, foreigners, wealthy businessmen, and small local grocers who represent the epitome of the adaptable trading spirit of the Arab world. The local Berbers (and also the rural inhabitants) occupy mostly the mountainous countryside. The Berbers, who claim to be of European descent because of their fair pigmentation and their blue or green eyes, originally called themselves Amaziah. It was the Romans who first called them *Barbarus,* from which comes the word *Berbers.* There are three distinct Berbers: the Ruffians of the north, the Chleuhs of the Middle and High Atlas, and the Soussi of the southwest. Within their local community, the Berbers derive their primary social identity from membership in a specific linguistic section; however, Berber identity could be easily lost if an individual settled with his family away from the indigenous group. Today, most Moroccans are of mixed ancestry between the Berbers, Arabs, and Africans. These admixtures have produced the varied Arabic dialects found in the country.

Most of the ancestors of modern Morocco's Jews (often called the Sephardi or Sepharadhi) arrived after the Christian reconquest of Arab-controlled Spain in the late fifteenth century. Others, however, were originally Berber speakers but later converted to Judaism and lived in various parts of the country—either in predominantly rural Jewish villages or as single families or small groups in non-Jewish families. Some of the Sephardi lived in special Jewish quarters called *mellah.* Others settled in cities, generally entering fast-paced businesses including artisan trade, illegal currency exchange, and trade in precious materials such as silver, gold, and diamonds. Although the Moroccan Jews have control over a significant portion of the economy, their population has remained small, partly because of immigration to Israel after it was created in 1948. More recently, Moroccan independence in 1956 and the increase in Pan-Arabic consciousness have combined to force a huge population of Jews out of Morocco.

A considerable but rapidly dwindling European community comprising the French, Spanish, and British and other Westerners live in the big cities, too. Many are expatriates employed by the government as teachers, technicians, corporate business managers, and so on. Their role in managing the economy of the country is crucial.

Moroccans of Berber-Arab descent have some unique and distinct characteristics that easily distinguish them from their neighbors. They are sometimes blue-eyed, with a variety of skin coloring due to generations of intermarriage, and are typically tall and thin, features that enables them to trek good distances. Moroccan women love gorgeous-looking clothes and they take time to adorn their bodies with body ink or dye, jewelry, and other forms of ornamental decorations.

LANGUAGES

The three major languages in Morocco are Arabic, Berber, and French. The official language, spoken by more than 70 percent of the population, is Arabic. The Berber speakers make up about 30 percent of the population.

French is the main language of business, government, and international relations. The school curriculum reserves an important place for the learning of the French language to promote interaction with the non-Arab world. Language is said to be the "principal determinate of ethnicity" even after centuries of miscegenation.[3] Arabic speakers are regarded as Arab and Berber speakers as Berber, regardless of their actual blood heritage. Berber, which belongs to the Afro-Asiatic language family, is encountered in different local tongues, but the three principal dialects include Tarifit, spoken near Al Hocema; Tachelhi, which is predominant in the southwestern region near Agadir, northeast of Marrakech, and east of the Draa Valley; and Tamazight, which is spoken in the Central Atlas region. Before the Arab invasion of North Africa in the seventh century, Berber was the dominant language spoken across North African. Today, the various local tongues have been mostly consigned to the mountain and dessert areas of Morocco. Having developed no writing culture, a common problem with speakers of most indigenous African languages, the Berbers lack the cohesive identity that a language can help create. Because written messages must be transmitted in another language, the indigenous tongue has been undergoing a process of corruption (or Arabization) as many Arabic words make their way into everyday usage. All sacred terms and the language of classroom instructions, for example, are mostly drawn from Arabic rather than Berber language.

Arabic, the most dominant form of language in North Africa and most of the Middle East, is one of the most historical languages in the world, widely recognized in the ancient cuneiform records of Mesopotamia. Its classical (Modern Standard Arabic) and popular (Moroccan Arabic) forms are spoken in the inner cities, plains, and mountains of Morocco. Modern Standard Arabic, the language of the Quran, is widely used throughout the contemporary Arab world. In Morocco, it is used in newspapers, correspondence, news broadcasts, speeches, and for most higher learning, especially in philosophy and religious studies, but rarely in conversation. Moroccan Arabic is the common language of the majority. Other Arabic speakers, with the possible exception of Algerians and Tunisians, find it somewhat difficult to comprehend Morocco's colloquial Arabic. Although Arabic has greatly influenced Berber life and customs, the indigenous culture has, in turn, influenced the pronunciation of classical Arabic in Morocco more than elsewhere in the Muslim world.

French is used in government circles and the cities. Despite the government's attempt to preserve the predominance of Arabic as the official language in Morocco since the end of colonialism in 1956, the use of French has proved somewhat indispensable. Great progress has been made toward Arabizing some institutions, but in other fields, a total change is not likely to occur. For instance, although Arabic is well suited to the writing of poetry and philosophical and religious texts, it is unsuitable for technical subjects. French will remain in use in businesses and factories for some time because politicians and civil servants find it useful to interact with Europeans and others in Francophone Africa. This has caused literacy in French to be acceptable among Arabic speakers. Additionally, about 20,000 Spanish speakers work in small organizations and centers in Morocco. Meanwhile, Arabic has continued to excel because the national educational philosophy is informed by the teachings of the Islamic holy book, the Quran.

EDUCATION

Government-funded education is free and compulsory from the age of 7 to 13, although the law obligating citizens to receive a certain level of literacy is not enforced. The 2004 literacy level was 51.7 percent of the population aged 15 years and older. The male-to-female literacy ratio is 64.1 percent to 39.4 percent. Although some families are strongly committed to the education of their female members, generally girls spend less time in school because their families often need them to assist the older women in their domestic tasks. Schools teach in Arabic until the third grade, after which bilingual education starts in both Arabic and French. After secondary school, the ratio of female-to-male enrollment drops sharply, often standing at 3 percent to 5 percent. University education is highly valued because it holds the promise of raising individual social status and standard of living, but the wealthy have a privileged access to higher education. The percentage of school enrollment for Moroccans has been on the increase since the 1980s. Among the most popular universities in Morocco are the University of Rabat and the Islamic Karouine University. Invariably, improvement in education has resulted in creating more economic opportunities, especially for the young people flocking to the cities.

CITIES

Cities have become more powerful in size and influence as increasing population and economic development tend to complement each other. With an annual influx of people estimated at 7 percent, Casablanca is the nation's most populous city and is the chief port city. With its high-rise buildings and beautiful historical Arabic architecture, the city combines the glamour of a modern city with the curious charm of an ancient Arab world. The harbor of Casablanca is one of the most modern in Africa. Rabat, the capital of Morocco, is the second largest city. The northern city of Tangier, one of Morocco's popular travel destinations, presents a picturesque and peaceful community near the Strait of Gibraltar. It is a huge tourist attraction and is considered high profile in some places because many artists and authors reside there. The former colonial coastal cities of Casablanca, Rabat, Tangier, Kenitra, and Safi are centers of industry and commerce. They have large foreign populations and are also the favorite destinations of rural migrants. The modern sections of these cities are carefully laid out with broad avenues, parks, and tall buildings. The neighboring ancient Muslim and Jewish quarters (called medina and *mellah,* respectively) are usually crowded, with low mud-brick houses along narrow, twisting alleys. Close to the modern cities, including Casablanca and Rabat, are shantytowns *(bidonvilles),* agglomerations of makeshift shacks, frequently built of flattened oil drums, bits of lumber, and corrugated iron, in which the poorest and most recent rural migrants take shelter.

RESOURCES, OCCUPATIONS, AND ECONOMY

Morocco is blessed with arable land, abundant water with fish and salt deposits, and generous quantities of phosphates and other minerals such as iron ore, manganese, lead, and zinc. Its scenic beauty has also made a vigorous and ongoing tourist trade possible. The economic potential of these resources partially explain why the control of Morocco was desired by foreign powers. Morocco's modern economy consists of industries such as mining, food processing, leather goods, textiles, construction, and tourism. Grain, citrus, wine grapes, and olives are grown commercially. About 50 percent of the population work in the agricultural sector, 35 percent in the service industry, and 15 percent in industry. The per capita income of Morocco is approximately U.S.$4,000.

According to a 2005 estimate, Morocco has an unemployment rate of 23 percent.[4] Most of the population can find only casual, seasonal, or itinerant jobs, and there is no state-sponsored employment insurance or social security benefits for the unemployed. Unemployment has led to the establishment of several male and female brothels in the big cities, particularly in Casablanca and Marrakech. Although there is a growing middle class, the gap between the rich and the poor has widened, thereby provoking increasing social unrest and food riots, which became rampant in the 1980s.

Like most African economies, Morocco's economy is largely agricultural, despite the government's ambitious quest to develop industry. As the government attempts to modernize the agricultural economy, farmers are gradually changing from traditional practices to more effective, mechanized methods. The arable lands support the production of cereal crops such as barley, wheat, and corn. Other significant cash crops include different types of citrus fruits, wine, vegetables, and olives. Moroccans also raise livestock to meet their domestic needs. The developing industrial sector provides a large number of jobs. Morocco is one of the world's leading producers of phosphates. Due to the high number of bodies of water in the area, fishing has become a prosperous industry. Meanwhile, the government is constantly encouraging small businesses to continue with its policy of diversification and industrialization. Tourism is also a huge factor in the economy, thanks to the country's great beaches and historical monuments.

GOVERNMENT

The present government in Morocco may be described as a constitutional monarchy. King Mohammed VI, the head of government, succeeded his late father, King Hassan II, on July 23, 1999. The king appoints the prime minister, following legislative elections, and also chooses the Council of Ministers. Driss Jettou, was appointed prime minister on October 9, 2002. In his first national address shortly after his father's death, Mohammed VI declared his commitment to the constitutional monarchy, political pluralism, and economic liberalism. He promised to tackle poverty and corruption, create jobs, and address Morocco's poor human rights record. Early indications suggested that the new king was serious about his depoliticization program. In a move that was widely held as populist, Mohammed VI shunned the glamour of his father's numerous royal palaces and disposed of a number of the royal limousines. Although these initial steps endeared Mohammed VI to many of the country's reformers and young people, many Islamic conservatives strongly opposed his liberal pretensions. Other critics also questioned his ability to uphold human rights and free speech. All these adjustments, turns, and twists are best understood in light of Morocco's long history of dynastic conquests, imperial rule, and religious conversions.

HISTORY

Early History

The historical evolution and development of Morocco has been marked by different groups of settlers and conflicts. This region of Africa is quite remarkable for its distinctiveness and role as the center of several medieval empires that at various times controlled much of North Africa and the southern parts of Spain. Unlike much of North Africa, Morocco did not fall under Ottoman Turkish rule in the sixteenth century. The remarkably brief period of the French and Spanish protectorates (1912–1956), during which tribal resistance was succeeded by Moroccan nationalism that produced by such leaders as Allal al Fassi, may be seen simply as a hiatus in the long history of modern Morocco.

Cave-dwelling people from the prehistoric Stone Age (c. 40,000–25,000 B.C.E.) originally inhabited the area of Africa now called Morocco. The remains of a Neanderthal boy were discovered in a cave near Rabat during a 1933 excavation. It is estimated that this boy, about 16 years old, lived approximately 50,000 years ago. At that time, this region was a dense forest occupied by lions, panthers, giraffes, ostriches, elephants, and antelopes. Rock drawings that date from 8000–5000 B.C.E. also affirm that a Neolithic culture flourished here until the Sahara region began to desiccate as a result of climatic changes that began after 2000 B.C.E.

The indigenous Berbers, who belong to the broad Afro-Asiatic–speaking peoples, entered the Maghreb around the Rif and Atlas Mountains early in the second millennium B.C.E. when the Neolithic invaders came in contact with the Bafots, a dark-skinned people, and remnants of the earlier Savannah people, who occupied the surrounding oasis. With no distinct name or geopolitics, the Berbers associated themselves primarily with family villages. The various villages competed with each other for the available resource control, especially the limited grazing grounds. Collectively they called themselves Amaziah (or *imazighan*), which means "free men."

Evidence indicates that in the twelfth century B.C.E., the Phoenician merchants arrived from their chief cities of Tyre and Sidon on the western coasts of Mediterranean and established trading posts at such places as Tangier, Ceuta, Melilla, and Tétouan. Later, people from Carthage (Kart-hadsht, or "New Town")—a town founded by the Phoenicians in about 814 B.C.E. in what is now Tunisia—tried to claim the northernmost region of Morocco. Neither of these foreign powers moved into the hinterland, but they traded with the Berber herders and farmers at coastal points.

In 146 B.C.E. after Rome plundered Carthage and laid waste to its people and their resources, Roman influence began to spread rapidly throughout northwestern Africa. For the next two centuries, the Romans administered the areas of present-day Rabat, Fès, and Taza, which they called the Province of Mauretania Tingitana, with its capital at Tingis (now Tangier). The Latin word *Mauretania* meant the land of the Moors—from which the name Morocco is derived. The Romans, who established colonies in Morocco, described the indigenous Berbers as an intractable people who gave their legions constant trouble.

In the third century C.E. the Romans were compelled to withdraw their political authority over Morocco as a result of dynastic crisis at home and relentless Berber pressure. This left the Roman influence in Morocco limited to only

Arch in Volubilis, the ruins of an ancient Roman city. Courtesy of Valerie Orlando.

Tangier, then administered by the empire's authority in Spain. One significant influence of Roman rule in Morocco is that many Berbers accepted Christianity, which they adopted in a hope to overcome the imperial authority from within. In the fourth century C.E., Christianity was made a state religion, and four bishoprics were established in Morocco. Also, Judaism won more converts as one of the oldest religions in Morocco. Although some Jews came to Morocco with the earlier Punic wars (264–241 B.C.E. and 218–201 B.C.E.), others arrived after the destruction of Jerusalem by the Roman army led by General Titus in 70 C.E. The Berber versions of Christianity and Judaism incorporated some elements of the indigenous religion.

In 429 C.E. the Gothic Vandals of eastern Germany overran the Roman-Christian army commanded by Castinus and soon took control of North Africa, including Morocco. As a form of resistance, the Berbers became nomads in an attempt to escape the atrocities wrought by the Vandals. The camel, which was brought to northwestern Africa by the Romans in about 200 B.C.E., helped to make Berber nomadic life a lot easier. Between 533 C.E. and 534 C.E., the Byzantine successors to the Roman Empire defeated the Vandals and tried to restore the prestige of Christianity as an imperial religion. But this new order had limited success because the independent-minded Berbers were averse to a new imperial master whose authority was restricted to scattered cities and fortified outposts. By the seventh century, as European political hold weakened, North Africans began to turn their focus away from

Columns in Volubilis. Courtesy of Valerie Orlando.

the ancient European empires. In effect, what resulted was the meeting of the indigenous Berber culture with the culture of Arabs under the vehicle of the Islamic faith.

The Coming of Arabs and Islam

In 681 C.E., Sidi Uqba (or Okba) ben Nafi led the first Arab raids into Morocco through the Taza highway and into the plains in an attempt to convert the Berbers (whom they saw as infidels) to Islam by the sword *(besiff)*. For years, Berber resistance delayed Arab control and total conversion. Eventually, in 710, Arab armies led by Musa (or Mousa) Ibn Nusayr, the governor of Islamized Tunisia (then known as Ifriquiya), succeeded in capturing and converting the Berbers of the plains and northern cities but not the Jewish inhabitants of Morocco. Once converted, the local Berbers formed the bulk of the army that invaded Spain in 710 C.E. They took control of most of the Iberian Peninsula under the Umayyad dynasty in Damascus.

Around 785, a recurring doctrinal rift between the Shia and Sunni sects of Islam led to the establishment of the first dynasty, the Idrissi (788–987), in Morocco. Idris Ibn Abdullah (died 791), a great-great-grandson of Ali (son-in-law of the Prophet Muhammad and the fourth succeeding caliph to Muhammad), fled to Morocco after a defeat by the Sunni supporters of Ali's rival, Muawiya, a leader of a powerful branch of Muhammad's kinsmen, the

Quarish (or Quraysh) family of Mecca. The founder of the Idrissi dynasty, known as Idrissi I, was known for his piety and charisma and enthusiastically welcomed by the Berbers. Some of the major landmarks of the dynasty included the establishment of the city of Fès between 807 and 808 C.E. and the founding of the popular Kairouyine University of Fès, one of the leading centers of learning in the world. The Idrissi dynasty began to wind down shortly after it was divided between the various sons of Idriss II in 987 C.E. While some of the new rulers maintained control of their respective principalities, others devoted their time to the enthronement of a more orthodox Islam within their spheres of influence. As a result, the Idrissi rulers became politically irrelevant. The political vacuum created by this development was quickly filled by two rival groups—the Fatimids and the Umayyads—between whom political power, in most parts of Morocco, revolved until the coming of the Almoravids.

The Almoravid dynasty (c. 1061–1147) ruled for about 86 years. It was the first of three Berber dynasties that ruled Morocco during the Islamic era, which began around 622 C.E. when the Prophet Muhammad fled from Mecca (a journey known as the Hegira). At its peak, this dynasty extended its power from northwestern Africa to Algiers (capital of modern Algeria). The Almoravids also dominated parts of southern Spain. After the Almoravid's power faded, the Almohads displaced them.

The Almohad dynasty (c. 1148–1269) ruled for about 121 years. At its peak, the Almohads turned Morocco into a Muslim empire whose frontiers encompassed what is today Algeria, Tunisia, Libya, and large parts of Spain and Portugal. By 1148, Abdel el Moumin, one of its greatest leaders, had secured control of all of Morocco, extending the territories of his empire far beyond the boundaries of his predecessors. Between 1160 and 1210, great architecture and industry, particularly weaving in silk, flourished in Morocco. Additionally, gold coins were produced as a medium of exchange. By 1230, this dynasty was growing weaker and its dominion shrinking in the face of challenges mounted by local dissidents. In desperation, the caliph accepted an offer of 12,000 Christian soldiers from King Ferdinand of Castile and León to help crush local dissidents and reclaim Marrakech from the rebels. In exchange for this favor, the ruler granted the Europeans permission to construct a Catholic Church in Marrakech. Eventually, the Merinid dynasty succeeded the Almohads in 1248.

Although the Merinid ruler had been jostling for power since 1146, they effectively took control of Morocco around 1248 when Abou Yahya moved his capital from Rabat to Fès. One of its notable leaders, Abou el Hassan, popularly known as the Black Sultan (reigned 1331–1351), ruled with an iron hand. After his death, his son ruled until 1358, when his opponents strangled him. From this point, the reigns of succeeding young sultans were marked by anarchy, coinciding with the Spanish and Portuguese expulsion of the Muslims from Spain. Many of the Moors who fled Spain established enclaves along Morocco's Mediterranean coast. The Merinid rulers were compelled by the victorious Spanish and Portuguese forces to compromise. Expectedly, the Merinid dynasty drifted into a state of prolonged decline, and its subjects were upset about the way their rulers yielded to Christian demands, including loss of control over the lucrative trans-Saharan gold trade with the emergence of the Atlantic trade as an alternative route to western Sudan. Moroccans generally view this era as a time of tyranny and oppression at the hands of foreign invaders. As is often the case with colonial domination, the presence of the Europeans revived Berber resistance against the pervading Arab presence in the Maghreb.

The Wattasid (or Ouatassids) dynasty (c. 1465–1550) came to power shortly before the beginning of the Spanish Inquisition in 1478. Mohammed Al-Burtughali, the sultan of the Wattas (Wattasids) reigned at Fès, whereas local tribal authorities and Sufi orders held authority over the rest of the country. The Wattasids established a chain of Islamic colleges to promote teaching and learning in the empire. In 1492 an influx of both Jews and Moors fled the Inquisition in Spain. The influx of the refugees increased the local population and benefited both the economy and the culture of Morocco. In this period, artistic and architectural traditions flourished in Morocco as the Moors introduced the kingdom to new intellectual and creative ideas. Some of the greatest architecture, fountains, mosques, courts, and buildings—both public and residential—were constructed during this period. By the mid-sixteenth century, the Wattasid dynasty was clearly under a threat of disintegration. Its greatest enemies were the Sa'adians, who seized control of Marrakech.

The Sa'adi dynasty (c. 1555–1668) more or less became a force to reckon with in 1525 when they seized control of Marrakech as a dissident faction. The Sa'adians eventually overthrew the Wattasids in 1557 and successfully took total control of Morocco. It was the first Arab dynasty since the fall of the Idrissids in 987 c.e. The Sa'adians are mostly remembered for driving out the Christians and organizing the Central Government (Makhzen). The Makhzen has survived as a sociopolitical legacy with little changes today.

The Alawi (or Alaouites) dynasty (1666–present), the current rulers of Morocco, ascended the throne in 1666. Sultan Moulay Ismail (ruled 1672–1727), one of the most popular rulers of the dynasty, was in power for 55 years. As soon as he ascended the throne, Ismail chose Meknès as his capital, and under him, Morocco experienced a period of prosperity. The sultan, who is primarily remembered for his flamboyant lifestyle, built palaces, mosques, terraces, gardens, shops, and fountains. Some of his legacies also included acquisition of hundreds of concubines and nearly 1,000 children, including 700 sons. Ismail was also known for his brutal reputation and bad temper. He was known to kill slaves on the spot if he thought their performance was substandard.

European Colonialism and Independence

European territorial incursion into North Africa gained momentum as Muslim power began to wane in the late fourteenth century. In 1399, the Castilians (of Spain) occupied Tétouan, and in 1415 the Portuguese wrestled Ceuta from Ottoman control and introduced Portuguese and Spanish influence over the coastal regions of Morocco. Gradually, the Portuguese gained control of most of Morocco's Atlantic coast and left Spain with a number of enclaves on the Mediterranean coast. In 1492, Spain, under rulers Ferdinand V and Isabella I, reclaimed Granada, a former Muslim stronghold. Thousands of Spanish Muslims and Jews either fled or were deported to Morocco, where many of them later gained influence in government and commerce. In 1578, the Moroccans defeated the invaders, and in the seventeenth century they successfully recovered control of most of the coastal cities.

By the beginning of second half of the nineteenth century, however, Morocco was becoming increasingly weak and isolated and was unable to withstand the challenges of European colonial overtures and successfully defend its long-standing history of organized society. Trouble began in 1894 when Abd el Aziz (ruled 1894–1908) ascended to the throne and began squandering of the country's treasury on luxuries. This reckless style of leadership made Morocco vulnerable to foreign control when Aziz accepted a loan from France to solve his country's financial problems. His brother and successor, Moulay Hafid (ruled 1908–1912), who overthrew Aziz in 1908, was forced to sign the Protectorate Treaty with France in 1912. The treaty granted France power over Morocco's foreign affairs and defense, and the southern part of Morocco (known today as Western Sahara) was placed under Spanish control.

The Moroccan people were upset with foreign domination of their affairs. Consequently, the Berber warrior groups launched a war of resistance against the European colonial presence, and France could not restore order until 1934. The first French resident general, Marshal Lyautey (1854–1934), recognized that the Moroccan government and culture should be respected. He also acknowledged that it was crucial to incorporate the younger generation in the modernization of Morocco, or disaster could result as they became frustrated and rebellious.

The resident generals who came after Lyautey did not share the same vision of respect for the indigenous culture. They soon turned Morocco into a virtual colony, controlling all aspects of the country's affairs and sidelining the traditional ruling class. At one point, the sultan was so alienated from power that he had to read the French newspapers to find out what was going on in his own land. Expectedly, an independence movement against French colonialism emerged in Fès in the 1930s and blossomed through the 1940s. It was met with violence and repression, but ultimately Morocco won its independence on March 2, 1956. In 1963, Morocco's first constitution was written. It guaranteed basic democratic freedoms and provided for an elected parliament but still granted the king substantial power.

Postcolonial Morocco experienced many challenges as it underwent many changes. For instance, the sultan changed his title to king. On the international scene, Morocco joined the Arab League and helped found the Organization of African Unity (now known as the African Union) in 1963. Additionally, the relationships between Morocco and France and Spain—its former colonial masters—have held, despite periodic diplomatic conflicts.

Although positive changes took place, much political unrest occurred throughout the 1960s and 1970s, including a number of attempted coups d'état. A stiff rejection of the 1963 constitution, despite a second draft by the opposition, forced King Hassan II to declare a state of emergency in 1965 and further entrench his autocratic rule. Also in the 1960s and 1970s, Moroccans and Algerians fought over border issues. In 1975, the lingering question over the sovereignty of Western Sahara, which Morocco claimed in the historic Green March in November, sparked conflict between Morocco and Algeria. Spain had hurriedly transferred its control over Western Sahara to Morocco and Mauritania to avoid a costly anticolonial war as the Polisario nationalist group prepared for an armed confrontation. The manner in which Spain arbitrarily transferred the sovereignty of its former colony to Morocco upset Algeria, and a war broke out between Morocco and its close neighbor. The war ended in a cease-fire with a proposal for a self-determination referendum in which the people of Western Sahara would choose to become independent or remain a part of Morocco. Relations between Morocco and Algeria were restored in 1988.

The war with Algeria forged unity among Moroccans. In 1984, parliamentary elections, held to further the democratization process in Morocco, established a constitutional monarchy. In 1998, a narrow majority elected Abderrahmane Youssoufi, a socialist leader and former dissident exiled to France, as prime minister. This election demonstrated accommodative spirit by King Hassan II and was widely welcomed as an example of democracy in action in Morocco, with expectations for further democratic openings.[5]

In 1999 Mohammed ben Al Hassan succeeded his father to the throne as King Mohammed VI. The new king, who is still in power, increased the pace of democratization and liberalization. Many exiled dissidents were allowed to return to Morocco. More evidence of his open policies was the 2000 march of 40,000 women in support of increased rights for women. More than just political changes are taking place, however. Presently, Morocco is seeking foreign investment and economic development. They have more than 100 enterprises, including two breweries, a winemaking company, and 11 luxury hotels. Outside of Islam, the main influence active in Morocco is Western cultural and economic styles, particularly in the urban areas where the modern world has made inroads into the indigenous culture. The government has initiated many policies geared toward claiming Morocco's place in the global community. There are trade deals to manage and arguments with other nations about access to the resources of the sea. There are also policies dealing with typical modern world issues such as population growth, equal rights, literacy, access to health care, and so on.

CULTURAL ISSUES

King Hassan II metaphorically described the mixed cultural heritage of Morocco as a tree whose roots lay in Africa but whose leaves breathe in European air. This may be an ideal depiction of the society if the "tree" approximates the most influential and long-lasting force in modern Moroccan society. Indeed, although the European cultural influences have remained remarkable, Muslim ideology and customs permeate Moroccan life. Islamic ideas and worldview dominate the ways millions of Moroccans explain reality, understand how the country works, relate to other members of the society, react to events and changes, and reflect on and even predict their future and that of their country.

The European cultural influences introduced by the Spanish to the northern and southern extremities of the country remain considerably important. The impact of French colonialism is more visible in the military, civil service, and modern sectors of the economy, political parties, and the general governmental structures. The French language continues to be widely used by the governing elite and the commercial interests, even though Arabic has been constitutionally designated as the official language since 1962.

NOTES

1. See Dale F. Eickelman, *Moroccan Islam: Tradition and Society in a Pilgrimage Center* (Austin: University of Texas Press, 1942), 16; American University Foreign

Area Studies Division (FASD), *Area Handbook for Morocco* (Washington, D.C.: U.S. Government Printing Office, 1966), 51.

2. The Moors of Morocco mostly descended from the Spanish Moors. They live mostly in the towns and big cities and have acquired wealth through commerce.

3. See, for instance, Harold D. Nelson (ed.), *Morocco: A Country Study* (Washington, D.C.: American University Press, 1985), 101.

4. Wayne Edge, *Global Studies: Africa,* 11th ed. (Dubuque, IA: McGraw-Hill, 2006), 135.

5. Abdeslam M. Maghraoui, "Depolitization in the Arab World? Depolitization in Morocco," *Journal of Democracy* 13, no. 4 (October 2002): 25–32.

2

Religion and Worldview

ISLAMIC RELIGIOUS IDEALS AND worldview permeate all aspects of social order in Morocco. Islam, which means "submission," effects the attitude of the great majority of Moroccans toward social action, their comprehension of reality, governmental power and authority, interpersonal and group relationships, reaction to events and changes, and how they reflect on and even foresee their future and that of their country. Article 6 of the Moroccan constitution identifies Islam as the state religion *(al-Islam din ad-dawla),* and nearly 98.7 percent of Moroccans are Muslims. Other small minority religions, such as Christianity (1.1 percent) and Judaism (0.2 percent), are tolerated to a certain degree.

Given its predominance in Morocco, the Islamic ideologies structure frames of reference against which "natural attitudes and behaviors" toward the world (worldview) are constructed. Religion, as identified by the famous philosopher Karl Marx (1818–1883), is the "opium of the masses." It often fulfills emotional, psychological, and even material wants. It can be used to explain human existence and help understand the complexities of life. Moroccans also turn to religion to deal with problems of insecurity, troubled relationships, witchcraft, and other sufferings of life, such as unemployment, poverty, sickness, and death. Human trials move people to seek solutions and remedies through prescribed rituals and adherence to the existing taboos, norms, and values that define their cosmology. A people's worldview or cosmology determines key concepts in which social actions and behaviors coalesce. In Morocco, as in every society, these natural impulses are transmitted to the young members of the society through a process of socialization. As individuals relate to society and tackle the realities of their life challenges, they tend to adopt new ideas and introduce fresh meanings on inherited values. This may result in conversions to new doctrinal orientations, as in the case of the Arab-Berbers who have been compelled by their historical experience to reshape their belief systems and ritual practices since the seventh century. To make religious ideas and worldview in Morocco more intelligible, the basic tenets of the Islamic religion will be highlighted first here because they offer the believer a comprehensive meaning to life. In some places, these overlap with the indigenous Berber belief system and practices. Thus, understanding this complexity gives a complete worldview of Moroccans.

WORLDVIEW

In Islam there is no separation of the sacred from the profane. The ultimate essence of life is to please God (Allah) through obedience to his will to attain the reward of paradise after death. Because the spiritual in Islam both detects and renews the temporal, creed and deed are like two sides of the same coin; hence, Islam is appropriately acknowledged as a total religion. Muslims are expected to be community oriented—that is, to be their brothers' keeper. Although not written in the Quran (the holy book of Islam), as are the Ten Commandments in the Bible, the five pillars in Islam (i.e., the cardinal articles of the faith) exert enormous influence on all aspects of society. These fundamental beliefs and practices, which must be honored for believers to attain the reward of paradise, are derived from both the Quran and the recorded lifetime practices (known as Sunna) of the Prophet Muhammad as observed by his close relations and acquaintances. The Quran is compiled from the recorded sayings and activities of the Prophet. These recorded sayings and activities are also called the Hadith. The Sunna constitutes the basic ideal in Muslim behavior. Muslims, including Moroccans, who strictly adhere to the traditions of the Prophet, are known are Sunnis. The other major sect in Islam, known as the Shiites (*shiat Ali,* or the party of Ali), currently accounts for about 15 percent of all Muslims in the world.[1] The Shiites also adhere to the traditions of the Prophet but fundamentally disagree with the Sunnis on succession. The five pillars in Islam include the Islamic testimony *(shahada),* daily prayer *(salat),* almsgiving *(zakat),* fasting *(sawm),* and pilgrimage (hajj).

Islamic testimony *(shahada)* is similar in importance to the Apostles Creed in Christianity. *Shahada* reaffirms the basic belief in the unity and oneness of God. This verbal profession is also known as *tawhid.* As an Islamist emphasizes, for Muslims, God is "beyond distinction and division and has no equal or associate."[2] Therefore, the Quran enjoins Muslims to serve no other gods but Allah to avoid the shame resulting from corruption of spiritual morals and destruction. Believers hold the Prophet Muhammad as the last and most outstanding messenger of Allah to whom the Holy Scriptures (Quran) were revealed. In strict Muslim practice, the Islamic testimony is supposed to be

> the first thing that a child should have uttered in its ear and the last thing that a dying person should hear. Parents may begin to teach their children how to speak by repeating the *shahada* as a father utters *"Allahu Akbar"* (God is all Great) and *"Ashadu anu la Allah ila Allah"* (I bear witness that there is no deity but Allah).[3]

The testimony of belief in the divine unity and oneness of God serves as the introductory message for each of the five daily prayer calls in Islam.

Prayer *(salat)* in Islam commences with a recitation of "the testimony of belief," or *tawhid.* Muslims are obligated to recite their prayers five times daily, at dawn, midday, midafternoon, sunset, and nightfall. In typical Islamic societies, mosques *(masjid),* the Muslim place of worship, are strategically located in all neighborhoods. Like Sunday Christian worships, Muslims' Friday congregational prayers are considered a good form of adoration, although it is not compulsory that everyone regularly participate. Believers are encouraged to recite their prayers wherever they are during each of the five daily calls to prayers. Women are not expected to regularly participate in prayers inside mosques. This is because a congregation of both sexes is commonly perceived as a source of distraction from the intended center of attention on God. A leader of prayer (Imam), who faces the direction of Mecca (the mihrab), leads Friday communal worships.

Fasting *(sawn),* usually observed in the month of Ramadan lasts for an entire lunar month of 29 days. The specific days of Ramadan are unfixed because of the lunar calendar and occurs at different seasons in different years. This period is generally perceived as a time for believers to resist worldly attractions. It reminds Muslims of God's revelation of the Quran to the Prophet Muhammad. All Muslims, with the exception of the ill, the young, travelers, and pregnant women, are expected to participate in Ramadan by abstaining from food, drink, tobacco, and sex during daytime hours as a way of promoting personal spiritual discipline. The Ramadan fasting commences each day with a prayer and a light meal usually prepared before sunrise. At sunset, family members gather to break the day's fast over dinner. In this way, Ramadan also serves as a time of family reunion and sacrifice. It challenges Muslims to share in the burden of the less privileged and to demonstrate unity through acts of piety.

Almsgiving (*zakat* or *sadaqa*) is reverence of God as well as an act of service to the Islamic community *(umma)*. Predicated on the existence of economic inequality, Islam demands that every Muslim help the needy and strengthen faith through generous material gifts. This religious tax of about 2 to 3 percent on one's accrued assets is similar to the Christian tithe. One of the noblest forms of *zakat* is that given secretly to the needy. Certain charitable gifts *(waqf)* can be in the form of endowments dedicated to the honor of God. In some Muslim countries, *zakat* has become a state-imposed compulsory alms tax or "pious endowments" and have become a popular indicator of a successful Islamic government, including Saudi Arabia, Libya, Kuwait, Bahrain, Pakistan, Sudan, and Iran. In the past, pious endowments in Morocco have provided funds for the ritual circumcision of orphaned boys, provided clothing and food to the needy, paid for the burial of the poor and strangers, and financed the marriages of destitute subjects. Today, the system focuses mostly on provision and maintenance of the religious infrastructures in the country.

The annual pilgrimage (hajj) to the holy places of Mecca and Medina, in Saudi Arabia, comes after the festivities of Ramadan, between the 8th and 13th of the 12th month of the Muslim lunar calendar, Dhu al-Hijja. At least once in their lifetime, believers who can afford the costs are obligated to perform a pilgrimage to Mecca. The Ka'aba, a small stone building holding the black stone given to Abraham by the Angel Gabriel, is at the heart of the hajj. The Ka'aba symbolizes God's covenant with Abraham's son Ismail, who is believed to be the ancestor of all peoples of Arab descent and, by extension, the Muslims. Male pilgrims at the holy sites must cover their heads and dress in a seamless white garment *(ihram)*. Like everyday prayer, the pilgrimage commences with the Islamic testimony and continues with a recital saying, "Here I am O God at thy Command! Thou art without associate." Pilgrims then proceed to the Ka'aba—Hebrew equivalent of the Holy of Holies or Christian tabernacle of the Eucharist. Although not an object of worship, at the Ka'aba, pilgrims may touch or kiss the black stone, as did the Prophet Muhammad, while they circle the stone seven times. Pilgrims must also resist engaging in sexual relations throughout the period. Among other activities, they stone three pillars that symbolize evil and Satan, and they visit the plain of Arafat, where they stand for hours before God and ask for divine mercy for all Muslims. On the third day, all pilgrims give ram, sheep, or goat sacrifices in commemoration of Abraham's unflinching willingness to sacrifice his only son, Isaac, to God. Muslims all over the world join in this festival called the Great Feast, or Eid al-Kabir or Eid al Adha (Festival of Sacrifice), by offering their own animal sacrifices. On the return from the pilgrimage, the men will earn the title *al hajj* and the women *al haja*. These titles come with expectations of a higher moral behavior. It requires the holder to practice fairness, respect, and honesty. It also forbids adultery, gambling, usury, drinking of blood, drinking of alcohol, and eating of pork. Muslims believe that the performance of the pilgrimage rituals has the benefit of spiritual healing and renewal.

Although not part of the five pillars, some Muslims now consider jihad, Arabic for "striving" or "struggle," as the "sixth pillar" of Islam. The essence of jihad is that Muslims must vigorously promote the cause of their religion. This should be done by acts of verbal persuasion, exemplary work, personal demonstration of spiritual force, and by war when the occasion demands. In this context, warfare becomes a sacred duty, and those who die in the cause of a jihad are promised the reward of paradise as martyrs *(shahid)* to their faith. In reality, a true jihad is rarely justified because Muslim factions often engage in wars to achieve vested interests.

Generally, the Quran, like the Bible, teaches the existence of guardian angels, resurrection and life after death, and heaven and hell. Islamic doctrine teaches believers to respect and show kindness to their parents and to eschew adultery. Muslims are also cautioned against covetousness and murder, although the latter is permitted with a just cause. In commerce, Muslims must give full measure and weigh with even scales. According to the teachings of the Prophet, which parallels the Golden Rule, a true believer must do unto others that which he desires for himself. In Islam, wealth not accumulated through usury, gambling, prostitution, and other such vices is considered divine. Poverty is seen as the work of the devil. Additionally, the enslavement of fellow Muslims is forbidden, as are lust, homosexuality, idolatry, and immodest attire for women. Also prohibited are the use of alcohol, gambling, suicide, and eating of pork or other animals that are not killed in accordance with Muslim rites.

The foregoing is an overview of the essence of religion and worldview in Islam. Although Muslims everywhere generally hold the teachings of the Prophet Muhammad as divine, there are differences in the practical observances of these doctrines between individuals, sects, and countries. These divergences simply mirror the influence of local culture and historical factors within the different Muslim communities across the world. In Morocco, the pre-Islamic indigenous Berber belief systems and practices have blended with the tenets of the Islamic religion to produce a unique brand of Islam in practice today.

INDIGENOUS RELIGIONS AND CHANGE

Although much of the indigenous Berber culture and belief systems have been interwoven with Arab Islamic culture and history, some surviving remnants of the local practices are still visible. Arab conquest of Morocco in the seventh century and the subsequent conversion of the local Berbers to Islam did not automatically result in a total destruction of the local culture. This is more the case when the majority of the intruding Arabs stayed in the more fertile coastal cities, whereas the local Berbers continued with their usual ways of life on the steppe, mountainous Rif, western and middle Atlas mountains, the oases of the Sahara, and other difficult-to-access locations. Even after centuries of assimilation through intermarriage, systemic Arabization, and exercise of central authority, elements of difference between the local and the imperial religion have proved resilient. This difference is evident in the brands of Islam practiced by the predominantly Arab urbanites and the largely Berber rural inhabitants. Scholars, however, have shown little interest in understanding the pre-Islamic indigenous religions of the Berbers. Among other problems of study is the lack of a pre-Islamic indigenous writing culture in which Berber culture would have been preserved. Even with the introduction of Arabic and Western forms of writing, early foreign scholars—and often exponents of the now discredited "hametic hypothesis"—systematically downplayed African history and cultural achievements by assigning every significant element of culture found on the continent to foreign influence.[4] The dramatic and overzealous Berber acceptance of Islam after initial resistance also did not help in preserving an unadulterated account of their religious traditions. The Berber response to Islam may have sprung from the crisis that followed the defeat of their ancient ancestral gods by Islam. The Berber apparently saw the discernibly successful alien religion as a ready weapon that could be adopted to redress the sociopolitical order in their favor.[5] Contrasts between the urban and rural forms of Islamic practices in Morocco can be drawn.

In the cities, the religious observances follow the stricter orthodox form of Islam commonly associated with many Arab states. For instance, restrictions exist on female movement and dress, although these restrictions seem to be decreasing with time. As the educated urban elite gained employment in modern industries and other Western-style institutions, increasing secularity became the trend. Although many devout Muslims still live in the cities, the emergent Westernized class of professionals is gradually dropping its strict observance of religious duties.

In the countryside, where Berber culture is predominant, Islam has mixed with local customs to form a unique amalgam of Quranic practices, with pre-Islamic belief in brotherhoods (*agurram;* plural, *agurramen*), the veneration of local saints, belief in the existence of spirits (djinns) and the evil eye *(dhittawin ta'affanain),* and other unorthodox ritual practices. Women, alienated from public practices of mainstream Islam and political power, particularly have

Berber woman of Errachidea. Courtesy of Valerie Orlando.

clung to these hybrid cultural traditions and, as such, continue to pass them to the younger members of their families.

Religion in pre-Islamic Berber society followed a common pattern found in most African societies. The traditional African religious practices are generally characterized by beliefs in spirits, deities, and gods that demand rituals, sacrifices, annual ceremonies, and other activities. Similarly, the Berbers believed in the existence of a special group of spiritual beings called djinns, whose supernatural powers can be used for either benevolent or malevolent purposes. In this light, the people sought protection from the evil djinns with magical incantations, petitions, offerings, animal sacrifices, and the use of objects believed to be fortified with special holiness *(baraka),* such as gunpowder, iron, and salt.

The origin of the belief in the djinns among the Berbers of North Africa cannot be exactly pinpointed. What is clear, however, is that this tradition developed outside the influence of a similar pre-Islamic Arab belief in the existence of spirits that infiltrated Islam from 632 c.e. The similarity in name found in the Berber and Arab spirits may be attributed to centuries of cross-cultural exchanges between the people of North Africa and their Middle Eastern neighbors. As well, the Berber practices were largely similar to those found in precolonial Guinea, Mali, Sudan, and Hausaland in Nigeria. The West Africans, often commonly referred to by the ancient Berbers as Guineans, were particularly known in North Africa for their expertise in exorcizing demons.

In Morocco, the belief in spirits pervaded every aspect of life. The abodes of the djinns included any conceived space, such as underground caves, mountains, valleys, hills, the air, rivers, seas, trees, and so on. The most common belief is that Satan *(iblis)* is the chief of the evil spirits. The belief in the existence of Satan, however, conjures less fear in the minds of people than do the lesser but more mischievous demons.

Much of what historians know today about the indigenous Berber religious tradition is because of the Swedish scholar Edward Westermarck, whose pioneering anthropological studies of the early 1900s remain a guiding light.[6] According to his work, among the djinns of Morocco, the most prominent is named Aisa Qandaisa. This spirit is distinctly from others of Oriental derivation. A prominent characteristic of Qandaisa is her libidinousness. She lives in rivers, springs, or the sea and is believed to be the old goddess of love, similar to the Moorish *jenniya,* which has a most disreputable character. In the Rif region and Dukkala (or Doukkala), situated on the banks of the Omm-Erbegh River, the folklore contains stories of marriage and sexual intercourse between men and the female spirits *djinniyas.*

In Berber folklore, the djinns are said to act like human beings in various respects, even when they have no bodies. They can enter anywhere anytime, and they speak with a thin voice. These spirits may assume different forms, including monsters, black men, stones, and animal shapes such as goat, sheep, frog, tortoise, and dog. The columns of sand and dust, which often pass through the plains of southern Morocco, were perceived as the handiwork of malevolent djinns. If a person stumbled in the dark, it was believed that he or she had trampled on a djinn. In recent times, the familiar phrase "In the name of God, the merciful and compassionate" *(Bismillah r-rahim)* is recited to keep the dangerous evil beings at bay. In the Andjra area of the Rif Mountains, the belief was held that the evil spirits pushed murderers to take lives. Even today, some people still believe that violent manifestation of disorders such as convulsion, epileptic and paralytic fits, and mental illness or epidemics such as cholera and measles *(buhamrum)* are the handiwork of diabolical spirits.

Westermarck's anthropological study has further revealed that evil djinns are believed to promote the practice of witchcraft *(shor),* a belief commonly shared in most parts of sub-Saharan Africa. One example of this belief is that the power of the djinns could be used by an enemy to set others in discord with their families, friends, or fellow workers. The ritual involves killing a black hen and shaving its head with a razor. A charm containing names of djinns is written on the head of the hen with its own blood. The head is then thrown into the adversary's house or workplace, and it is believed that within three days the malevolent spirits invoked in the ritual will set the targeted individuals or group against one another.[7]

In a traditional African universe where humans and spirits shared a common space, it was natural that men and women found ways to guard themselves and their belongings against fiendish attacks. Some of the ways designed to guard against attacks from such wicked spirits included the burning of candles, putting salt in or underneath pillows, and wearing amulets made of pieces of iron, steel, silver, and brass. Today in Morocco, reciting passages from the Quran has become one of the most efficacious weapons against demonic attacks. This practice highlights an aspect of the adaptations between the Islamic religion and the indigenous culture.

The belief in djinns is also closely connected with the dread of the "evil eye." The evils caused by them are largely the same as those mentioned previously, as are the classes of persons particularly exposed to them and the charms used against them. As another anthropological study illustrates, the evil eyes emanates from the belief that people can cause others harm by conceiving evil in their minds, which brings on the malevolent spirits against the object and causes the harm that is intended to befall the person or thing upon whom the evil eye has been cast.[8] In Fès, certain passages of the Quran have been found helpful as a protection against the evil eye. This again shows the overlay of Islamic rituals on indigenous practices and how this blend has produced a unique form of Islam found in Morocco.

The relations between men and spirits, however, are sometimes pleasant. It is believed that those who possess the power can use the services of the spirits for their own purposes. In the Souss (or Sus) region, including the capital Agadir, for instance, some holy men are believed to use the power of words in the Quran to manipulate the strength of the djinns. Other holy men are believed to possess the power to open a closed door without a key. Similar to divination in African traditional religion, some magicians *(hokama)* from Souss are believed to find buried treasures with the help of the djinns. Such acts of divination also may be deployed to apprehend criminals, to get news about an absent member of the family, or to inquire about the fate of a sick person at home. According to a detailed study, there are occasions during harvest seasons when farmers induce the djinns with sacrifices to give special holiness *(baraka)* to the grains. In Aglu, for example, part of harvest may involve the farmer slaughtering a sheep to increase the *baraka* contained in his grain. The animal sacrifice is made in honor of the master of the threshing floor *(lmluk unrar),* who is addressed as follows: "Master of the threshing floor, look here, we killed for you" *(Lmlik unrar, hayyagg ngrars fillaun).*[9]

The foregoing elucidates a striking religiosity common in most African indigenous societies. The Berbers, like other African peoples, are gregarious; the family often holds property in common, and a man can call upon the services of his fellow villagers for certain purposes, such as the building of a house, clearing of farmland, and so on. The community often makes provision for the poor. An insightful study of the Aith Waryaghar and the Ibuqquyen, two local Berber communities of the Rif region, notes that every individual belongs to an aggregate, which shapes his or her allegiances; at the same time, each person is autonomous and seeks to maximize options. Every life event is subject to the condition that "if God so wills" *(insha-allah)*. As this study further explains, underlying contracts is the premise that certainty is controlled by God and not by humans.[10]

Islam and Social Change

In general, Islam retained some aspects of the pre-Islamic Arabic belief in small gods and spirits. The Prophet Muhammad recognized the existence of these gods in ancient Meccan society but classed them among the demons. Apparently, the benevolent spirits were adopted into the world of Islam, whereas the malevolent ones were classified as opponents of Allah. Hence, the Quran stands as a powerful antidote to their activities. Centuries after the introduction of Islam, the Berbers have retained certain elements of their culture, although these customs have been reproduced and given new meaning.

Berber culture is intricately premised on ritual ceremonies and symbolism. With the challenges of their harsh, semiarid, and mountainous environment, the Berbers rely on natural rituals to survive and give meaning to everyday life. As a result, the Berbers, although they identify with the Islamic religion, do not often adhere strictly to the set observances. It is not uncommon to find a Berber who could not resist the temptation of a daytime feast or indulgence in alcohol during the month of Ramadan fasting. Cults of saintly veneration tend to attract more serious devotion among the Berbers, and it is common to find descendants establishing communities around the tombs of departed holy men. Almost every village in Morocco has its saint or prophet, and arguments as to their relative sanctity and powers sometimes provoke intervillage conflicts.

Holy Men and Saints

A close connection exists between the belief in the existence of spirits and the notion of individuals endowed with holiness or divine blessings. In this cosmology, it is believed that saints have control over both the good and the bad spirits, and they assist saints in performing their miracles. In this context, the spirits act as the servants of the saints as well as of living men. As a detailed study on the folk religion notes, the concept of holy men in Moroccan religion is similar to that in European Christianity. The religious reverence of local holy men tends to peak after their death, and all relics associated with them,

King Mohammed V's mausoleum in Rabat. Courtesy of Valerie
Orlando.

including their tombs *(kubba),* are elevated to the same saintly status. The
local people conceive such holy men as their patron and protector saints. It
is, therefore, common for individuals troubled by various forms of hardships
and tragedies, such as sudden and frequent deaths in families, barrenness, and
unemployment, to visit the tombs of the local saints to ask for their special
blessings and intercessions.[11]

Most neighborhoods and communities have their different patron saints.
In Fès and Meknès for instance, Mulay Idris and Sidi Muhammad ben Isa,
respectively, are among the most popular saints. Sometimes urban migrants
come to their host communities along with their local saints; others simply
adopt a new cult or resuscitate a weak one. A good example of the latter situ-
ation in encountered in Casablanca, where the growing number of shantytowns *(bidonvilles)* and suburbs have absorbed the rural communities along
with their patron saints.

The veneration of saints is widespread among the uneducated, particularly the rural and urban poor, and among many urban middle-class women.
Saintly veneration has witnessed a long-term decline in the cities, probably
because of the increasing impact of Western education and influence, the
general secularization of life, and the greater tendency toward orthodoxy
among reform-minded city dwellers.

Government attitude toward the cult of saints could be described as benevolent tolerance. For instance, in the late 1960s, King Hassan II turned the

tomb of his father, King Mohammed V, into one of the most symbolic sites of power and saintly veneration in Morocco. This symbolism is sustained by the claims of the present ruling dynasty, the Alaouites, to descent from the lineage of the Prophet Muhammad.

Similarly, the descendants of other key saints *(awlad siyyid)* often use their claim to holy ancestry to corner special privileges. These lineages, as care-takers of the tombs and shrines of Marabouts, receive contributions from pilgrims and devotees of these saints. Over the years, the traditional Islamic concept of pilgrimage to Mecca has been widely reinterpreted in the popular culture to include pilgrimage to shrines of the saints. Some Berber-Arabs of the Rif Mountains equate seven pilgrimages to the shrines of Mulay Idris at Fès to a pilgrimage to Mecca.

Belief in the hagiography of saints is institutionalized in strong cults of brotherhoods still existing in Morocco. In the traditional Berber society, net-works of brotherhoods serve as a symbol of identity for all those who profess loyalty to a particular patron saint. As an aspect of popular culture, the leaders of these brotherhoods enjoy enormous political and religious influence.

Networks of Brotherhoods

Networks of brotherhoods loyal to pious men or holy people have devel-oped to be a prominent part of Islam in Morocco. These holy men are called Sufi, apparently because they often dress in woolen *(suf)* attire. The ninth and tenth centuries witnessed the rise of prominent Sufi leaders who attracted many followers because of their teachings, assumed the ability to cure con-ditions such as epilepsy, exorcised those possessed by demons, and led a simple lifestyle, which easily identified with the poor. In Morocco, Sufism soon became popular because it was easily adaptable to certain aspects of the indigenous Berber traditions. Thus, as the leaders of the old mystical order championed the conversion of fellow Berbers, a corruption of the faith seemed inevitable. By retaining elements of their indigenous belief systems and practices, the form of Islam preached from the start was already tend-ing toward Islam's mystical *(tariqa)* path. Across North Africa and Western Sudan, these brotherhoods built their cult of loyalties around local saints or masters who were believed to show the "way" as chosen guides.

Islam, as preached among the brotherhoods, continued to reinforce the authority of the local elite as their disciples sought to win God's favor through their spiritual masters or guides. Similar to the kind of reverence for saints in the Catholic Church, Muslims in Morocco believe that some divine grace is granted to ordinary mortals who come in contact with indi-viduals and objects that possess divine holiness *(baraka)*. Although this form of belief is in conflict with orthodox Islam, the conformist Islamic teachers (ulema) have no choice but to accommodate them. Today, the old brotherhood system continues to exist in Morocco, despite attempts to rid the faith of it. Their evident success and social utility rests in the fact that people run to them in times of crisis. Thus, the orders came to exercise significant political influence in Morocco.

RELIGION AND POLITICS

Islam disapproves of the rule of non-Muslims over the community of believers *(umma)*. In Morocco, as in other Islamic states, the political leader must also be able to lead the faithful. The Quran prescribes the unity of the individual, state, and society under the all-powerful will of God. Islamic rulers exercise both temporal and religious authority, and the Western idea of separation of church and state appears irrational. Islamic countries like Morocco are theoretically divided into three domains. All Muslims collectively form the abode of Islam *(Dar al Islam)*. The People of the Scripture—the adherents of other revealed monotheistic religions, Judaism and Christianity—are allowed to practice their religion as "protected people" *(dhimmis)*. Polytheists are consigned as people in darkness needing of salvation. Accordingly, the people are designated as either citizens, in the case of Muslims, or subjects—all others who do not practice the faith. These designations come with all the accoutrements of power and privilege.

To obtain legitimacy, the leader of the Islamic community must demonstrate attributes of holiness and charisma. The leader is believed to impart some of this blessedness to the people and to objects with which he comes in contact. It is commonly accepted that the predisposition to special holiness or blessings runs in families, hence monarchical governments rule most Islamic countries. Expectedly, the Prophet Muhammad is believed to have the most charisma and holiness. Therefore, his descendents (the *shaifa*) are highly respected because they are believed to have inherited many divine blessings from the great Prophet of Islam. In the past, some Berbers who are possibly descended from the original Arabs have tried to assert their claims of sainthood and sharifian descent with varying degrees of success. The claim of the royal family of Morocco to be descendants of the Prophet Muhammad accords the current king, Mohammed VI, an overarching respect, authority, and legitimacy among his people.

Similarly, in the various regions predominantly inhabited by Berbers, the notions of holiness and charisma *(baraka)* equally serve as crucial sources of leadership and legitimacy. Individuals who appear to be endowed with great holiness are looked up to as leaders of society. Often, the Muslim monks or hermits or holy men (Marabouts), especially those reputed to have extraordinary spiritual power, are in open opposition to the authority of the sultanate. These local leaders still recognize the superior blessedness of their king and national leader.

Although Islamic ideas dominate all aspects of life in Morocco, the teachings of Judaism and Christianity are acknowledged as the basis of the Muslim faith. Therefore, it is imperative to briefly look at the nature of power relations between the overwhelming Muslim majority (98.7 percent) and members of the minority religions, Christianity and Judaism, which together account for 1.3 percent of the total population.

CHRISTIANITY

Christianity, as a monotheistic religion, figures prominently in Islamic belief systems and practices. Before Islam, the Romans, and later the Byzantines, had introduced Christianity in the area today called Morocco. The German Vandals, who dominated the North African region from 430 C.E., expended every effort to obliterate the Christian heritage in Morocco.[12] Whereas the Vandals hounded the Catholics and destroyed their churches, they favored the Jews and granted them freedom of religious expression. The Byzantines defeated the Vandals in 553 C.E. and tried to restore the authority of the Catholic Church in Morocco. This effort met with Berber indifference, and therefore little success was made until the arrival of the Arabs in the seventh century.

Today, Christianity in Morocco is chiefly the religion of French, Spanish, and other European settlers or recent immigrants. Approximately 350,000 Christians, both foreigners and locals, live in Morocco. The past two decades have seen only a very small number of new converts through the activities of foreign missionaries—particularly those of the Roman Catholic Church, which was established in Morocco in the nineteenth century. Roman Catho-lic archdioceses are located in Rabat, the national capital, and Tangier, the northernmost city, which have a long history of European contact. Casablanca and Fès are among the other big cities that also have congregations. The local authorities and media are not enthusiastic about renewing the Christian faith in Morocco, but they encourage the founding of Western-style schools, hos-pitals, dispensaries, and other institutions.

Generally, the minority Christians are regarded as second-class citizens, and this social classification comes with limited opportunities. For instance, although there is no existing law permitting employers to know employees' religious backgrounds as a condition for employment, some employers have all the same tried to discriminate against their non-Muslim employees. In terms of opportunities, most Christians going into private business lack access to much-needed capital. Some Christian neighborhoods also count among the most deplorable ghettos. As a result of this marginalization, young Christians are forced to migrate to the big cities or overseas in search of better opportunities. All these problems have combined to curb the growth of the local church. Thus Christianity in modern Morocco is restricted to the European immigrants, who, despite their strategic importance in the modern economy, are theoretically viewed as "the protected people."

JUDAISM

Judaism, Islam, and Christianity are monotheistic religions. Moroccan Jews form the largest Jewish community in the Arab world. The Jewish presence in Morocco has been a subject of controversy even though the earliest evidence of a Jewish presence in northern Morocco is found on tombstones dated from the second century C.E. Many of the Jews moved into Morocco from Carthage (Tunisia) along the Mediterranean coast. Others arrived from the area known today as Libya. They easily mixed with some local Berber groups in both Algeria and the mountains and oases of Morocco.

During the Reconquista of the sixth and seventh centuries, the Moroccan Jewish community increased as a result of incursions of Spanish Jews and mass conversions of Berber tribes. A large Jewish community of about 70,000 lived in Morocco until the late 1940s, when the state of Israel was created. This, together with the Arab-Israeli wars of the 1950s and 1960s, forced many Jews to leave Morocco in large numbers.

Although always subject to the authority of the sultan or king of Morocco, the Jews are granted administrative autonomy over their local community and institutions, including the rabbinic courts. Exceptions are obtained in cases involving legal disputes between Jews and Muslims, in which case the Islamic judicial code (Sharia) takes precedence. In Morocco, the powerful chief rabbi and rabbi-judges, known as *dayyanim,* serve as both spiritual and judicial leaders.

Over the centuries, the Moroccan Jews, like their Berber-Arab Muslim countrymen, have developed a tradition of rituals and pilgrimages to the tombs of holy men. Across Morocco, Muslim authorities recognize about 13 such sites. Every year on designated dates, Jews from around the world, including Israel, visit these graves. The grave of a particular pious rabbi of Moroccan origin, named Israel Abu-Hatseira, draws the largest number of pilgrims.

The Jewish community has undergone a profound change during its history, from relative freedom from abuses in the pre-Almohad (i.e., before 1150 C.E.)

dynasty in Morocco to intimidation and persecution after the ascendance of the Almohad ruler Abu Yusuf Y'aqub al Mansur (1184–1199). Nonetheless, the relationship between the Jews and the Muslims has remained relatively cordial even though it has endured occasional tensions.

Today, the Jews living in Morocco are fairly treated, although their exact political status has been debated. This state of affairs denotes the underlying process of a radical flux that characterizes the Jewish community in modern Morocco. For instance, the traditional Jewish homes called *mellahs* have conspicuously disappeared. The younger generation of Jews has rarely considered it desirable to live in Morocco because of their lower status and limited opportunities. Casablanca, Fès, Marrakech, Rabat, and Tangier still have synagogues, old-age homes, and Jewish restaurants, but it appears that the future existence of a substantial Jewish population in Morocco is unlikely. This more so, given the recent increase in Islamic militancy worldwide. The May 16, 2003, suicide attacks on four Jewish targets in Casablanca have not helped in assuring the Moroccan Jews that they are safe in this North African region.[13]

In general, the predominance of Islamic ideas and worldview in Morocco is a product of history, environment, government, and society. Over the centuries, Islam has interacted with both the indigenous Berber belief systems and elements of pre-Islamic Christianity and Judaism—all combining to produce the distinct form of Islam in practice today. Whereas Arabs and Berbers are profoundly Islamized, the prevalent social organizations of the latter do not reflect the unity envisioned by orthodox Islam. The religion, in a sense, is largely a natural and integral part of the individual rather than of the group. Both the Berbers and Arabs have retained and modified beliefs in holy men, saints, brotherhoods, spirits, and their accompanying rituals. These together have colored the worship of both the Muslim clerics and the Western-educated elite. The latter appears to be more sympathetic to the Christian and Jewish populations with whom they share mutual business interests. Islam in Morocco is indeed a superimposition of Quranic ritual and ethical principles on top of belief in spirits *(djinns)*, the evil eye, rites to assure good fortune, the practice of hagiography, and the increasing culture of globalization.

NOTES

1. This sect originated as a political movement supporting Ali (the cousin and son-in-law of the Prophet Muhammad) as the rightful leader of the Islamic world.

2. Ira G. Zepp Jr., *A Muslim Primer: Beginner's Guide to Islam,* 2nd ed. (Fayetteville: University of Arkansas Press, 2000), 31.

3. Carolyn Fluehr-Lobban, *Islamic Societies in Practice,* 2nd ed. (Gainesville: University Press of Florida, 2004), 35.

4. Until recently, the exponents of the hametic hypothesis claimed that Negro Africans were not capable of achievements on their own. In this view, they tried to see any important element of cultural, technological, and scientific achievements found in Africa as having been brought to the continent by other peoples of non-Negro origin.

5. Mervyns Hiskett, *The Course of Islam in Africa* (Edinburgh: Edinburgh University Press, 1994), 2.

6. Edward Westermarck, *The Belief in Spirits in Morocco* (Abo, Finland: Abo Akademi Press, 1920). This source provided the substance of the foregoing illustrations on local Berber religious practices.

7. Ibid., 115–116.

8. M. W. Hilton-Simpson, "Some Superstitions noted among the Shawia Berbers of the Auries Mountains and their Nomad Neighbors," *Folklore* 26 (1915): 228–234.

9. Westermarck, *Spirits in Morocco,* 118.

10. Roger Joseph and Terri Brint Joseph, *The Rose and the Thorn: Semiotic Structures in Morocco* (Tucson: University of Arizona Press, 1987), 13–17. See also David Montgomery Hart, *The Aith Waryaghar of the Moroccan Rif: An Ethnography and History* (Tucson: University of Arizona Press, 1978).

11. Richard F. Nyrop et al., *Area Handbook for Morocco* (Washington, D.C.: U.S. Government Printing Office, 1972), 91.

12. The Vandals are one of the eastern German groups comprising the Vandals, Visigoths, Ostrogoths, Lombards, and Burgundians. They were involved in the demise of the Roman Empire under their leader Gaiseric, who ruled between 428 and 477 C.E.

13. The terrorist attacks killed 28 bystanders and 13 suicide bombers who were believed to be part of the network linked to Osama bin Laden, the mastermind of the September 11, 2001, attacks on the World Trade Center and the Pentagon. There were no Jewish casualties in the Morocco attacks because they occurred on a Jewish holiday when the buildings were empty.

3

Literature and Media

Cocktail parties shock our festive customs;
Alien habits invaded thoughts and homes.[1]

—Mohammed Abu-Talib, 2003.

MOROCCANS HAVE EXPLORED THEIR multicultural Barbary, Jewish, Arabian, and European traditions to create impressive literary achievements. Mohammed Abu-Talib's (1930–2000) poetry, reprinted in 2003, aptly captures the sturdy Berber-Arabic cultural setting on which French colonialism (1912–1956) was superimposed. Before the arrival of Europeans, Arabic literary culture thrived in Morocco. The cosmopolitan and historic cities of Tangier, Fès, and Casablanca were popular for hosting world-class writers and poets whose works expressed ideas of universal interest. Many of these scholars carved out a niche for themselves in the field of Arabic literature, tapping into the rich oral traditions of Berber-Arabs. The dawn of European colonialism across the African continent brought new dimensions to what it meant to be literate. For the Moroccans, literacy also meant learning to read and write in French, but they did not discard their Islamic heritage. Rather, the old order gradually sought accommodation with the new. In the midcolonial era (1920–1939)— particularly from the 1930s—Moroccan poets and writers, by writing in French and later English, began to demonstrate strength of mind that has progressed toward a rediscovery of the country's position in the literary world.

As the colonial order aggrandized by strengthening its bureaucracy and mission schools, the Moroccans quickly picked up the rudiments of the white man's education, fashioning their newly acquired knowledge into a weapon of combat against colonialism. The emergent educated elite established nationalist newspapers, which they recognized as crucial in getting their ideology across to the less privileged masses whose support was, nonetheless, important for the achievement of the ultimate goal of independence. After independence in 1956, the media expanded with the establishment of more daily and weekly newspapers, magazines, periodicals, and radio and television stations. In 1993 the popular poet, essayist, and novelist Abdelhak Serhane's *Sun of the Obscure Ones (Le Soleil des Obscurs)* won the French Prize of the Arab World (Prix Français du Monde Arabe), which is the most prestigious prize for literature in the Arab world. The award symbolized a rediscovery of Morocco's long history of literary excellence, which had peaked during the Merinid (1146–1546) and Wattasid (1465–1546) dynasties.

To better understand Morocco's diverse and wide-ranging literary environment, it is important to explore literary works in Moroccan Arabic, classical Arabic, French, and English. Standard use, proper words, letters, and sounds have been developed for the unique Moroccan Arabic that is rarely spoken outside the country. This orthography has become a medium of education, socialization, historical preservation, scholarly inquiry, and cultural nationalism. Traditions preserved in oral literature have survived as new talents produce and reproduce both new and old ideas and others publish in Moroccan Arabic for targeted local readers. Accounts recorded in the classical Arabic language of 28 alphabetic letters, which differs from the Roman alphabet, still occupy a prominent place in Morocco. Meanwhile, the ability to produce creative works in French and English has launched some Moroccan authors to international acclaim as their works are now more readily accessible to an international readership. Early on, Western scholars and writers, such as Jean-Claude Blachere, Hamilton A. Gibb, Ernest Gellner, Clifford Geertz, and particularly Paul Bowles (who resided in Tangier for many years), helped bring Arabic literary tradition to the Western reader.[2] In Morocco, the most popular literature and television dramas are in classical Arabic or Moroccan Arabic, which is a combination of Arabic and the various indigenous Berber dialects. The reason for this is that it is easier to successfully communicate humor in a language commonly understood by the people. The new generation of North African writers now writes in one language and then have their works translated into one or more other languages to satisfy both local and international markets. The ability to transliterate from one language to the other has made the rich indigenous oral literature of Morocco readily available to the international audience.

ORAL LITERATURE

As one writer has stated, "folklore keeps the past alive."[3] The cultural traditions of the Berber-Arabs of North Africa are rich in this type of creative oral literature. Although at a diminishing level of patronage, the indigenous folklore has survived colonial assault. Moroccan folklore varies from area to area, and each tells a unique story. The annual Marrakech Festival of Morocco remains a bounty of literary culture and tradition.

Although oral literature is not as widespread as written works, storytelling remains one of the most common forms of education and entertainment in Morocco. In their different studies on oral literature in Morocco in particular and the Maghreb in general, some scholars have highlighted the role of mothers in storytelling and the transmission of culture to the younger generation. Through nighttime family stories, Moroccan women help in the formation of imageries that are often presented in modern literary writings.[4] As recently as the 1970s and 1980s—that is, before televisions became widespread—the professional itinerant storytellers *(hakawati)* frequented the open markets in Morocco, summoning their audience by the tap of drums. In an eyewitness account, in *The Voices of Marrakesh,* one observer offered a vivid description of storytelling in the 1970s in Morocco. According to this source, the storytellers usually drew the largest crowds at informal public gatherings. People gathered around them and were never in a hurry to leave.

> Their performances are lengthy; an inner ring of listeners squat on the ground.... Others standing, form an outer ring; they, too, hardly move, spellbound by their storyteller's words and gestures. Sometimes two of them recite in turn. Their words come from further off and hang longer in the air than those of ordinary people.... In honor of their words, storytellers wore striking clothes. They were always dressed differently from their listeners.... They gave the impression of exalted yet somewhat fairytale personages. They spared few glances for the people by whom they were surrounded. Their gaze was on their heroes, their characters.[5]

This depiction tells about the special expertise and intellectual abilities of the storytellers, who were gifted enough to hold their audience spellbound for hours. They carefully chose their stories and plotted the narratives to generate and sustain interest and curiosity. The listener not only wants to hear the end of the story, but also plans to catch the storyteller another day, if pleased by his performance. The content and context of a story may be changed or modified by the professional entertainer to reflect current issues, teach morality, and to satisfy his audience.

Exploiting his popularity and expertise for maximum rewards, the storyteller usually demands some form of monetary compensation from his listeners before beginning his story. As the story unfolds, the storyteller improvises a song that sums up the sequences of the completed parts of his narrative. He gauges the dept of interest and satisfaction his audience derived from his stories. If everything is going well, the storyteller may require his listeners to pay a second or even the third time to hear the end of his story. Often, the storytellers are also skillful drummers and singers—skills that go together with the profession. Otherwise, they hire the needed hands. For more effect, the stories are systematically interspersed with drum beats and prayers. Story topics are diverse, and the storyteller carefully determines his choice of topics in the same manner as a schoolteacher plans classroom instruction. Much of the folklore has connections with the good and bad spirits (djinns) and the casualties of evil eye. According to one study, such remedies as personal hygiene and burning of incense are often recommended.[6] Other topics dwell on social ills, animals and their unique qualities, famous scholar-saints, and ancient Berber-Arab heroes. The storytellers have woven tales about how common human problems and experiences came about. They offered answers as to why, for instance, the owl is a wise animal. Their stories also enlighten the listener on human wisdom, follies, and morality. A story on envy and malignant joy, for instance, may begin or end with an exhortation, "If there is much envy in Gharb, sell your property and go to India." This simple advice teaches one how to be mindful of the dangers of envy to personal safety. Famous saints such as al-Yusi and Mulay Isma'il are often the subject of these folktales. According to an expert, the legends of al-Yusi and Isma'il are popular in Morocco because they conform "to the classic theme of the virtuous saint overcoming an unjust ruler."[7]

Many aspects of Berber-Arab folklore have been integrated with mainstream written literature and historiography. A good example is the legend of Kahina, a North African heroine:

> No legend has been adopted, transformed, or used by as many social groups as the legend of Kahina.... It has reflected most of the modern ideologies in the Mediterranean and mirrored the early Islamic ideology and the medieval ideology of Islam, as well as modern ideologies in both Europe and Islam: colonial ideology, European anti-colonialism, Arab nationalism, North African nationalism, Berber nationalism, Zionism, and feminism.[8]

Indeed, this legend of Berber origin, which has been refashioned and reproduced to suit diverse purposes, illustrates how many aspects of the indigenous folklore have been successfully incorporated into the mainstream historiography.

Other aspects of the folklore have been recorded in creative writings, audiocassettes, and videos. Some important examples of such works of ethnography are those by Edward Westermarck and Ernest Gellner.[9] These authors and other recent writers have identified oral artistic expressions in a variety of genres: proverbs, songs, festivals, and oral narratives. Each of these forms describes and analyzes creativity, values, norms, traditions, and histories. They capture and explain changes in culture, the lives of eminent figures, social institutions, and practices. Above all, they aim to educate the younger generation and to prepare them for life's challenges.

Like their counterparts elsewhere, the premodern sovereigns of Morocco patronized poets and their works. Poetry is one of the most popular celebrations of kings, noblemen, and heroes. In the late thirteenth and fourteenth centuries, Leo Africanus and Ibn Khaldun—two geniuses who ranked among the greatest of North African historians—documented the thriving Moroccan mystics who produced certain kinds of poetic genres often considered unconventional in strict Muslim practice. According to Leo Africanus,

> It is not rare for some gentleman to invite to his festivities one of the masters among those principal Sufis (mystics) with all his disciples. When they arrive at the banquet, they begin by saying their prayers and singing hymns. Once the hymn is finished, the most aged begin to rend their garments and if, while dancing, one of these aged men falls, he is immediately raised up and set on foot again by one of the young Sufis, who frequently gives him a lascivious kiss.[10]

Besides poems created for merriment and conviviality, there are other categories associated with rituals, divinations, and rites of passage. A study on Rifian poetry revealed that the Berbers compose romantic poems in simple lyrics to gain the attention of women with singing and deliberate sexual movements. The poems, which aptly portray the people's everyday life, allow the poet to speak symbolically of love. Some of the poems depict the intention of a young woman to persuade her father not to force her into a marriage with a stranger; others are meant to alert men when a young woman is seeking a potential husband.[11] Poems among the Berber-Arabs are common and are encountered in diverse forms. Altogether, this category of poems, like music and dance, are more than mere artistic creation. Indeed, the poems are for pleasure as well as part of the social discourse and means of conferring influence and status. The upgrading of the various aspects of the indigenous oratory has, thus, offered enormous cultural resources upon which modern Morocco depends in constructing a common identity and inspiring its citizens.

LITERATURE IN BERBER AND ARABIC LANGUAGES

In Morocco, the coming of Islam in the seventh century and the introduction of a writing culture in Arabic language both encouraged and enriched the flourishing of a literary tradition that has continued to grow as new talents emerged. Arabic language promoted creative enterprise through a successful education system based on the Quran. Abd Allab Bib Yasin (died 1058) and his sectarian movement known as *al-Murabitun* (Almoravids) established a center for prayer and Islamic instruction in the eleventh century. Also, the establishment of numerous institutions of higher learning (madrassas) in Morocco, especially in the dynastic periods of the Merinids (1146–1546) and the Wattasids (1465–1549), attests to the success of Islamic education in the Maghreb. The madrassas in Morocco were particularly popular for their cosmopolitan outlook. The Muslim scholars and teachers *(ulama)* of this generation dedicated time to learning and writing in Islamic culture. The scope of their interests mirrored the drive of the predominantly Sufi religious order in Morocco to intellectual pursuits. Some examples of notable Arabic scholars of Morocco included Ibn Ajarrum, Abu'l-Hasan, Abu'lnan, and Abu Abdallah Ibn Battuta. Many foreign scholars, including legends such as Leo Africanus, Ibn Khaldun, and Ibn al-Khatib, found their peace residing in Morocco, particularly in Fès, Casablanca, and Tangier. In essence, when one talks about the literary traditions of Morocco in the precolonial era, it must be emphasized that this was a long historical practice comprising Middle Eastern, European (particularly Spanish Andalusia), Jewish, and indigenous Berber-African input.

Ajarrum (died 1322) was a Berber, born in the small town of Sefrou. According to a detailed study on the intellectual life in Fès during the reign of the Merinides, Ajarrum wrote a "treatise on grammar which, in one thousand verses (from which it takes its name of *Alfiya, alf* signifying one thousand) summarized the essentials of Arabic grammar."[12] Although underused today by students of Moroccan and Islamic studies, this document remains an important source of information on the development of writing in classical Arabic and Moroccan Arabic orthographies.

Among all the pious scholars (i.e., the *alem;* singular, *oulem* or *alim*) of the premodern Arab world, Abu Abdallah Ibn Battuta (1304–1377) of Morocco is widely acknowledged as the most traveled in world history, perhaps with the exception of the Italian explorer Marco Polo (1254–1324). The descendants of Battuta were rural Berbers of northern Morocco. His parents were professional jurists and judges who practiced their trade in Morocco and Andalusia (southern Spain). Battuta grew up in Tangier, where he was trained in juridical sciences, grammar, logic, rhetoric, law, and theology. Contemporary African historians owe a lot to Battuta's vivid eye-witness (although sometimes biased) accounts of life in medieval West and East Africa. Ever adventurous, Battuta visited the ancient Mali Empire between 1352 and 1354. As a Sufi (a believer in the mystical and ecstatic dimension of Islam), Battuta betrayed in his writings, *Travels in Asia and Africa 1325–1354* and *Ibn Battuta in Black Africa*—still one of the rare original sources of West African history—his astonishment with the cultural differences between his Morocco and the various western and eastern African societies he encountered during his travels.[13]

Abu'l-Hasan and Abu'lnan were scholarly princes, whose strong interests in Islamic learning saw the king's court almost in competition with the universities as the leading center of intellectual activities in premodern Morocco. According to Battuta, each morning the king usually gathered around him scholars and learned men with whom he conversed on topics of interest. Their favorite subjects of conversation often included verses from the Quran dealing with jurisprudence, mysticism, and poetry.[14] Leo Africanus, a contemporary of Ibn Battuta, added that the sovereigns of the Merinides dynasty of Morocco were proud sponsors of competitions in poetry, particularly on the anniversary of the Prophet Muhammad's birthday. As Africanus observed, "The reciter stood on a very high platform. Then following the judgment of competent persons, the king gave to the most highly esteemed poet one hundred pieces of gold, a horse, a female slave, and the garment that he was wearing. He had other pieces of gold given to all the others, so that all took leave of him with a reward."[15] This generous size of rewards attests to the immense respect the king's court held for intellectuals and literary creativity.

A critique of intellectual life in medieval Morocco and the Arab world, however, may include the pervading influence of Islam on ideas and thought as a shortcoming. Islam conceived the individual as a means of interpreting inspired knowledge. In this regard, most of the works of these scholars look alike—in the sense that many focus on Islamic religious issues—hence, contemporary and more secular writings have easily overtaken them in popularity. Yet, there are many timeless aspects of Arabic literature. Like the Christian Bible, the Quran, compiled more than 13 centuries ago, has continued to serve as a useful source of knowledge about mysticism, historical knowledge, social control, government, law, and jurisprudence. Above all, the Quran represents the critical interpretation of the prophetic texts and theology of the unity of God. Therefore, Arabic education and writing have remained a priority throughout Morocco. European colonialism brought new concepts and ideas that helped enrich and transform Morocco's literature and media.

Literature in French and English

French colonial policies in Morocco changed with time, and diverse objectives and goals drove European cultural imperialism in the country. Initially, French colonial education targeted only the indigenous Berbers. The Arabs were ignored because the Europeans thought the Islamic culture would help to preserve the peace and order necessary for colonial exploitation. Because Western education and Christianity opened new opportunities for employment in the colonial service and social mobility for the newly educated, however, Western education became equally desirable for many Moroccans of Arab descent who wanted to avoid alienation from the new colonial order. This drive resulted in an increasing taste for European ideas and institutions as well as the quest for freedom from colonial subordination.

In the late 1920s, modern Moroccan literature began an inchoate but historic transition from its Arabic audience to French and Western readership with the appearance of political essays and articles *(maqala)* in pamphlets and periodicals. By the end of the World War II in 1945, the new trend had entered a radical phase. Moroccan nationalist intellectuals such as Allal Al Fassi, Abd el Krim, Abdelkabir Khatibi, and Abdelkarim Ghellab had started gaining popularity for their nationalist writings in classical Arabic verses. These scholar-nationalists attacked capitalism and its bureaucratic institutions, which they perceived as slowing down the pace of decolonization. World War II had seriously injured French colonial pride, thereby providing new vehicles for articulating social and political thought in the context of increasing agitation for independence. Additionally, with the emergence of the Cold War (1944–1989), the East-West ideological struggle quickly attracted the fascination of most African authors, including their Moroccan counterparts. Across Africa, literature and creative writing became encapsulated in anticolonial undertones.

In August 1951, *Al Istiqlal* (Independence), a weekly tabloid of the Istiglal Party, began to publish nationalist commentaries in French. Expectedly, these anticolonial essays drew the ire of the French colonial officials as manifested in the temporary suspension of the Istiglal Party in 1952. Meanwhile, Mohammed A. Tazi's fiction attained a wide audience in the period of decolonization. Tazi's creative works represented an important period of change to new political ideas published in magazines like the *Signpost of Truth (Thawat al Haq),* also owned by the Istiqlal Party. Like most of their counterparts elsewhere, the nationalist writers defended the precolonial Arabic-Islamic social values and conservative literary trends. Another nationalist newspaper *The Speaker (The Aqlam),* published by the National Union of Popular Forces (*Union Nationale des Forces Populaires,* UNFP), also supported nationalist ideological essays and academic papers that promoted nationalist sentiments.[16] Nevertheless, imperial culture wrought a profound effect on Arabic literature. This effect has continued to manifest in varied forms such as lingering traces of dissent to adoption of Western institutions and styles, campaigns against monarchical authority, reform of Islam, and the struggle of women to free themselves from patriarchal control.

The recent trends have occupied the works of modern writers such as Driss Chraibi, Mohammed Abu-Talib, Abdelhak Serhane, and Mohammed Zefzaf. The emergent authors write about the cultural heritage of Morocco in particular and that of North Africa and the Middle East in general for their African, Muslim, and Western readers. Although they possess different levels of expertise and varieties of interests, these writers exhibit unity in many ways. Their works communicate a profound sense of duty to construe the sociopolitical changes of the postcolonial order. Their ability to communicate in Arabic, French, and recently in English demonstrates their implicit hunger to advertise their gifts of prose beyond the limited confines of the Arab world.

Driss Chraibi writes mostly in French, although he distorts the language rules and uses a disproportionate number of vulgarities as a distinct form of opposition to official literary expectations. The spirit of dissention that was formed in the colonial era remained a common character of postcolonial literature up to the 1980s and 1990s. One of the dominant themes of Chraibi's novels has been the call for sociopolitical reforms in postcolonial Morocco. Since the 1950s, Chraibi has been calling for resistance against outdated Islamic and Christian religious ideas, but his *Open Succession (Succession ouverte)*, published in 1962, diverted a bit from this focus with an economic history of French expatriate workers' lives in colonial Morocco.[17] Among Chraibi's most popular novels are *The Simple Past (Le passé simple)*, which came out in 1954 as an attack on patriarchal forms of control that he perceives as often reducing the voices of women and children to oppressive silence and obedience. In reference to paternal authority *(Le Seigneur)*, Chraibi observed that "any life other than his [father's] own … is annihilated."[18] In a recent collaboration with Gareth Stanton, *An Investigation with the Country (Une Enquette Au Pays)*, Chraibi depicts life in postcolonial Morocco as a continuation of the oppressive colonial system.[19]

Mohammed Abu-Talib emerged in the 1960s as one of the most popular Moroccan writers in English. Abu-Talib is largely seen as the initiator of English studies in Morocco. He helped shape English language and literature in Morocco through teaching, planning, administration, and scholarly writing. His works aim to enhance individual identity through historical and cultural dialectics of diversity. In his works, Abu-Talib speaks to the reality of cultural differences in the context of transformation and change. Abu-Talib is a benevolent social critic, and his poetry communicates social realities with an original touch of humanistic appeal and liberal doses of humor, notwithstanding the difficult task he chooses by trying to construe these works in an alien language.

One of the greatest revelations in recent times is Abdelhak Serhane who came into the limelight with his *First Draft (Messaouda),* published in 1983, which won the Literary Prize of the Free Radio *(Prix Littéraire des Radio Libres)* in 1984.[20] With a passion for criticizing social ills, Serhane's two major works, *Children of the Narrow Streets (Les enfants des rues étroites)* and *Sun of the Obscure Ones (Le Soleil des obscurs),* highlight some dysfunctional aspects of traditional society in Morocco that tend to disallow the young people the enabling environment for development and happiness.[21] This genre is further explored in *The Love to Circumcise (L'amour circoncis),* which dwells on circumcision and condemns acts of sexual pervasion, hypocrisy, and similar practices that are commonly encountered in Morocco even among those considered pious men.[22]

New literary stars such as Mohammed Zefzaf continue to appear in the educational institutions of Morocco. Zefzaf, a high school teacher, is widely considered to be the most prolific of contemporary fiction writers. He writes on any contemporary social issue. In 1970, Zefzaf published his controversial work entitled *The Woman and the Rose (Al-Mar-'ah wa Lwardah),* which was perceived by religious conservatives as too immoral and therefore potentially corruptive.[23] The author is also perceived as unpatriotic for his apparent positive views of Western culture over Arab or Maghrebi traditions.

POETRY

Poetry has always been important in Morocco, first as part of established indigenous tradition and later as a vibrant Arabic and English genre. Many poems are encountered as parts of a collection of selected literary pieces, passages, works of art, and music. Others appear in the print media and in academic magazines. The elegant poetic works of Paris-based Mohammed Khair Eddine (b. 1942) bear the hallmarks of the influence of French culture on modern literary forms. Eddine's poems focus on the need to change Moroccan customs and traditions, especially those concerned with monarchical and patriarchal authority and power. Eddine's long period of residence in France helped him shift from nationalistic ideological writings to a more artistic expression. His works and others of the same genre are published in *Soufflés (Blown),* a French-language literary review established in 1966.

Ahmed Sefrioui, a poet of Berber descent who writes in French, won respect with his unique depiction of everyday life in ethnographic novels. Particularly, *The Box of Miracles (La Boîte à Merveilles)*, which focused on the life of ordinary craftsmen in his hometown, Fès, was widely read in Morocco. Also, his collection of short stories, *The Garden of the Magic Spells, or, the Perfume of the Legends (Le jardin des sortilèges, ou, Le parfum des légendes)*, which was produced in the form of parables, received wide interest.[24]

Among the emerging writers, Ahmed Lemish, a high school teacher in Rabat, has drawn national recognition for his stubborn resolve to write poems in the local Moroccan Arabic rather than the more widely read classical Arabic or even French or English. For years, this resolve cost Lemish the respect and recognition he deserved among his intellectual cohorts in Morocco, despite his scholarly publications in literary journals. His recent work, *Who embroidered the water …!? (Shkun Trez Lma …!?)*, came as a successful surprise to his critics.[25]

In Morocco, most literary writers are men. Male writers primarily produce gender-biased narratives, focusing on male heroes and characters. The past three decades, however, have seen the emergence of female authors who have been contesting a rightful place for women in the history and development of Moroccan society.

FEMALE AUTHORS

Moroccan female writers deal more often with the contributions of women to the independence struggle of the 1940s and 1950s as well as to gender issues. One contemporary author revisited the "historiographic struggle that has taken place over Morocco's national liberation movement."[26] She shows how, in their quest for social change, Moroccan women have not only confronted gender-biased status legislation and the predominantly Islamic patriarchal forms of authority but also challenged the dominant historiography, especially with respect to the anticolonial struggle. Largely, feminist historiography aims to claim a rightful place for women in the mainstream history of contemporary Morocco.

Among these feminist writers is Leila Abouzeid, a graduate of the University of Texas at Austin and a pioneer female writer of literature translated into English. An accomplished fiction writer, Abouzeid used the style of traditional storytellers to relate events in her stories. Her first and most popular novel, *Year of the Elephant: A Moroccan Woman's Journey towards Independence*, presents women's perspective on contemporary problems of poverty, gender, divorce, and other family-related issues.[27] This work is also important for its demonstrated bravery in focusing on the forces of traditional culture and modernism, calling for a critical reevaluation of the meaning of independence from both the national and the individual standpoints. Abouzeid extended this topic in her *Return to Childhood,* which is a sort of personal experience of the impact of the Moroccan nationalist struggle of the 1950s on family order.[28] In her most recent work, the semiautobiographical *The Last Chapter,* Abouzeid tells about the struggles of a young Moroccan woman to gain identity in the new society under transition in the second half of the twentieth century. The author locates the interaction between the Western and traditional values in a shifting but conflicting context.[29]

Other contemporary female writers have also made their marks in poetry. For instance, Amina El Bakouri's poems are full of references to the Arabic poetic heritage. With striking success, Bakouri uses the complex interrelationship between different texts as a guide to literary interpretation. This original approach symbolizes a sort of recovery of Morocco's past poetic memory. Although Bakouri writes in classical Arabic, her poems are lucid, and the style oozes a spiritual aura.[30] Similarly, Toura Majdouline's unique natural style in *Leaves of Ash* and *The Weary* has won her respect.[31] The tone of her poems is serene and discreet. At the same time, the poems depict remarkable bravery, with a touch of simple and realistic representations.

Female authors focus on how the Moroccans themselves view, relate to, and represent their own culture. They challenge monarchical control and continuing patriarchal authority with a strong yearning for a truly free society, which was promised in the rhetoric of the anticolonial struggle. In this context, women's struggle in Morocco, as revealed in the recent historiography, represents a new phase in the continuing quest for a freer society. As the monarchy struggles with the dilemma of balancing privileged authority and power with democratic freedom, a more critical and vigorous press holds the promise to sustain the campaign for reforms.

NEWSPAPERS AND MAGAZINES

The Moroccan modern press dates back to the beginning of the colonial era. Between 1903 and 1923, the press, such as it was, served to consolidate the French colonial administration in Morocco. Gradually, the press developed in phases in response to both international events and nationalist movements. Press ownership has also transformed in phases from a mouthpiece of the colonial administration to a supporter of monarchical authority since independence. The latest development is the gradual emergence of private ownership of newspapers and magazines.

Generally, monarchical authority has created problems of freedom for the media in Morocco. The major government-owned newspapers include the dailies *Al Anbaa, Le Matin,* and *Assahra.* The government controls newspapers through bureaucratic supervision of news broadcasts and appointment of trusted managers of the media houses. Such governmental censorships have attracted both local and foreign condemnations. In 2003, for instance, the media rights organization Reporters Sans Frontières (Reporters without Borders), based in Paris, strongly condemned the habitual prying in the press by the intelligence services. It attacked Morocco's press law, which stipulates prison terms for writings that question the relevance of Islam in society, continued monarchical authority amid the new global quest for democratic institutions, or the legitimacy of Morocco's territorial claims over Western Sahara.

In spite of government censorship, recent strides have been recorded in the continuing expansion of the print media. Recent legislative openings have resulted in increases in the number of daily, weekly, and monthly newspaper houses in Morocco. In 2000, there were about 1,780 local and foreign newspapers in circulation. These newspapers and magazines cover a wide spectrum of interests—politics, religion, medicine, economy, sports, women, computers, arts, decoration, youth, education, and so on. They carry news items, editorials, advertisements, and columns, reflecting the gradual response of the sociopolitical space to the globalizing world order, with the monarchy demonstrating more tolerance to criticism and divergent views. A state statute of August 2, 1995, allows for expression of political ideas and sociocultural opinions within a defined press code, which empowers the minister of the interior to punish any publication considered offensive to government. As in all Islamic states, most Moroccan newspapers devote a front section to Islamic sermons. Low literacy levels limit newspaper readership, and competition among publishers for advertising is intense. Since 1999, Morocco's private press has gradually engaged in free debate on a number of previously taboo issues, including social problems.

RADIO AND TELEVISION

Local radio broadcasting began in Morocco in 1924 under the French colonial administration. After World War II, the government granted nationalists the freedom to establish radio broadcasting. Shortly before its independence, the French colonial authorities also established the first television station in Morocco in 1954. This was the first in the entire Arab world. In November 1958, the late King Mohammed V established the Maghreb Arab Press Agency (Maghreb abd Arabe Presse; MAP) with the motto "News is sacred, comment is freedom." The MAP has wide local and international outreach and is a leader in international news broadcasting in Morocco. Radio and TV broadcasting, like the print media, serve to educate, inform, and entertain the people. The expansion of the economy since the end of colonialism has made more radio and television sets available to the people, and the number of stations has increased.

A nationwide television network began broadcasting in 1962. As with the print media, the television stations are under governmental control. All materials shown on television usually pass through strictly bureaucratic surveillance. In the beginning, television relied on foreign programs and films. The Center for Moroccan Cinema (Centre for Cinématographique Marocain [CCM]), founded in 1944, influenced TV programs until independence in 1956, when the organization was turned over to the new government. The determined quest for the Arabization of education in postcolonial Morocco brought about a rediscovery of the place of folk performers, films, plays, and drama series produced mostly in the Arab world. While the CCM was undergoing a program of indigenization, Egypt provided an important source of films and other television programs. Today the CCM is still responsible for the promotion and regulation of the film industry, and the popularity of films made in Algeria and Morocco have since displaced their Egyptian competitors. The government uses television as a medium to propagate religious morality and encourage civic engagements. As a vehicle for transmitting education and culture, the stations, too, broadcast school programs. A recent study noted that television "generally thought of as placing few literary requirements on the viewer, now reaches the homes of Moroccans of all socioeconomic levels."[32] The Moroccan television industry continues to grow and to seek the means to adapt to its local milieu.

The focus of improvement in this sector has been on adaptation to new global technological improvements. Today, the electronic media covers nearly all parts of the country. The government-owned Moroccan Broadcasting Network, Radio-Television Marocaine (RTM), serves a wide range of audiences in Arabic, French, English, Spanish, and the three major Berber dialects—Tamazight, Tachelhit, and Tarifit. The government also retains a substantial control of Medi 1 (Radio Méditerranée International), based in Tangier. Medi 1 broadcasts programs in Arabic and French. The number of households that own radios and televisions has increased substantially since the early 1980. According to a 1999 U.S. Department of State estimate, the country has a 1:3 ratio of radio ownership and 1:6 ratio of television ownership.[33] Given that family sizes are usually large in Morocco, these figures imply that there is at least one radio and/or television per household. The moderate cost of satellite dishes has also enabled about 1.2 million viewers to access to a wide variety of foreign programs.

The government owns the two major television networks, RTM and 2M-TV, based in Casablanca. Meanwhile the government has expressed the intention to liberalize and privatize these state-owned media houses, but the plan may be a long time coming because the monarchy is mindful of the likely political costs of losing its control of the media. Altogether, about 35 television stations operate in Morocco, including the Western Sahara, where the National Radio (NR) and Saharan Arab Democratic Republic (SADR), launched in the 1970s, continue to serve the independent struggle of the Polisario Front. NR and SADR transmit news in Arabic and Spanish.

THE INTERNET

Despite a lack of consistent government policy for its development, Moroccans have boldly taken on the emerging trend in Internet access. Perhaps with the exception of South Africa and Nigeria, Morocco has one of the largest telecom sectors in Africa. Morocco has about half a million internet users, and the government can censor any Internet site, particularly those hostile to its policies on Western Sahara. Web users in Morocco can access information from offices and private homes.

NOTES

1. Mohammed Abu-Talib, "Drink to the Prophet," in Richard S. Harrel, William S. Caroll, and Mohammed Abu-Talib, *A Basic Course in Moroccan Arabic* (Washington, D.C.: Georgetown University Press, 2003).

2. For an erudite analysis on the works of Westerners who specialized in Arabic studies, see Roger Allen, *The Arabic Literary Heritage: The Developments of Its Genres and Criticism* (Cambridge: Cambridge University Press, 1998).

3. See Arthur Palmer Hudson, *Folklore Keeps the Past Alive* (Athens: University of Georgia Press, 1962).

4. See Zohra Mezgueldi, "Mother-word and French-language Moroccan writing," *Research in African Literatures* 27, no. 3 (fall 1996): 1–14; Heidi Abdel-Jaouad, "'Too Much in the Sons': Mothers and Impossible Alliances in Francophone Maghribian Writing," *Research in African Literatures* 27, no. 3 (fall 1996): 15–33.

5. Elias Canetti, *The Voices of Marrakesh: A Record of a Visit*, trans. J. A. Underwood (New York: Seabury Press, 1978), 77.

6. For an interesting account, see Norman A. Stillman, *The Language and Culture of the Jews of Sefrou, Morocco: An Ethnolinguistic Study* (Manchester, UK: University of Manchester Press, 1988).

7. Henry Munson Jr., *Religion and Power in Morocco* (New Haven, CT: Yale University Press, 1993), 190. For more on the common themes that dominate professional storytelling in Morocco, see Harold D. Nelson, ed., *Morocco: A Country Study*, 4th ed. (Washington, D.C.: American University Press, 1978), 138.

8. Abdelmajid Hannoum, *Colonial Histories, Post-Colonial Memories* (Portsmouth, NH: Heinemann, 2001), xv.

9. Edward Westermarck, *The Belief in Spirits in Morocco* (Abo, Finland: Abo Akademi Press, 1920); Edward Westermarck, *Ritual and Belief in Morocco* (London: n.p., 1926); Edward Westermarck, *Wit and Wisdom in Morocco: A Study of Native Proverbs* (London: Routledge, 1930); Ernest Gellner, *Saints of the Atlas* (Chicago: University of Chicago Press, 1969).

10. Leo Africanus, cited in Roger Le Tourneau, *Fez in the Age of the Marinides,* trans. Besse Alberta Clement (Norman: University of Oklahoma Press, 1961), 128.

11. Roger Joseph and Terri Brint Joseph, *The Rose and the Thorn: Semiotic Structures in Morocco* (Tucson: University of Arizona Press, 1987), 92.

12. Le Tourneau, *The Marinides,* 121–122.

13. Said Hamdun and Noel King, *Ibn Battuta in Black Africa* (Princeton, NJ: Markus Wiener, 1996), ix–xxxii, 1–12.

14. See Mahdi Agha Husain, "Manuscripts of Ibn Battuta's Rihla in Paris," *Journal of the Asiatic Society of Bengal* 20 (1954): 22–32; Mahdi Agha Husain, "Ibn Battuta, His Life and Work," *Indo-Iranica* 7 (1954): 6–13; G. H. Bousquet, "Ibn Battuta et les Institutions Musulmanes," *Studia Islamica* 24 (1966): 81–106.

15. Leo Africanus, cited in Tourneau, *The Marinides,* 127.

16. Nelson, *Morocco,* 136–137.

17. Driss Chraibi, *Succession ouverte* (Paris: Denoël, 1962).

18. See Driss Chraibi, *Le Passe Simple* (Paris: Denoël, 1954), 15; or see Driss Chraibi, *The Simple Past,* trans. Hugh A. Harter (Washington: Three Continents, 1990).

19. Driss Chraibi, *Une Enquette Au Pays* (Paris: Editions du Seuil, 1981).

20. Abdelhak Serhane, *Messaouda* (Paris: Editions du Seuil, 1983).

21. Abdelhak Serhane, *Les Enfants des rues etroites* (Paris: Editions du Seuil, 1986); Abdelhak Serhane, *Le Soleil des Obscurs* (Paris: Editions du Seuil, 1992).

22. Abdelhak Serhane, *L'amour circoncis* (Paris: Paris-Méditerranée, 2001).

232. Mohammed Zefzaf, *Al-Mar'a wa al-warda* [The Woman and the Rose] (Beirut: Al-Dar-al-Muttahida li al-Nashr, 1970).

24. Ahmed Sefrioui, *La Boîte a Merveilles* (Paris: Editions du Seuil, 1954); Ahmed Sefrioui, *Le jardin des sortilèges, ou, Le parfum des legends* (Paris: L'Harmattan, 1989).

25. Ahmed Lemish, *Shkun Trez Lma …!?* (n.p., 1994).

26. Liat Kozma, "Moroccan Women's Narrative of Liberation: The Passive Revolution?" in James McDougall (ed.), *Nation, Society and Culture in North Africa* (Portland OR: Frank Cass, 2003), 113.

27. Leila Abouzeid, *Year of the Elephant: A Moroccan Woman's Journey towards Independence* (Austin: University of Texas Press, 1990).

28. Leila Abouzeid, *Return to Childhood* (Austin: Center for Middle Eastern Studies, University of Texas, 1999).

29. See Leila Abouzeid, *The Last Chapter* (Cairo: American University Press, 2003).

30. Amina El Bakouri, *Ra'ian Ya'tika Lmadih* (Rabat: Sais Midit, 2002).

31. Touria Majdouline, *Leaves of Ash* (Rabat: Union of Moroccan Writers, 1990); Touria Majdouline, *The Weary* (Oujda, Morocco: Dar al Jusoor, 2000).

32. Daniel A. Wagner, *Literacy, Culture, and Development: Becoming Literate in Morocco* (Cambridge: Cambridge University Press, 1993), 36.

33. See also *Annuaire Statique du Maroc* [Annual Statistics of Morocco] (Rabat: Ministry of Communication, 1999, 2000).

4

Art and Architecture/Housing

ART AND ARCHITECTURE/HOUSING DESIGNS are expressive forms of the totality of Morocco's sociocultural heritage. They provide historians with a rich source of information on the people's civilization and the link between the past and present. Like other aspects of life in the kingdom, Moroccan art and architecture have been heavily influenced by Barbary, Arabic, Jewish, Roman, and European (particularly Spanish and French) cultures. In Morocco, artwork is found in traditional handicrafts produced in stone, silver and gold, fabric, leather and skin, wood, earthenware, ceramics, iron, and brass. Traditional architectural decorations are found mainly in the form of mosaics and murals. A mosaic is a form of surface decoration produced by arranging pieces of different colors to shape a desired pattern; murals are a decorative art applied to form an integral part of a wall or ceiling surface. Since independence in 1956, art and architecture in Morocco have been identified as crucial forms of cultural expression, identity formation, and nation building. In this regard, early in the 1960s, the government of King Hassan II (died 1999) established centers for artistic education that, among other things, aim to preserve the rich cultural heritage of the people and to expand on the country's lucrative tourist industry.

Given the diverse and dynamic roots of Morocco's cultural life, it is difficult to draw a clear line between the traditional, contemporary, or modern categories of art and architecture. Even more elusive is the notion of Berber, Arab, Jewish, Roman, or European models.[1] Each of these categories overlaps one another, and their histories cut across different cultures and historical eras. Therefore, it is more appropriate to state that Morocco's art and architecture are a harvest of cultural diversity. This hybridism makes Morocco an interesting subject of study. For analytical convenience, two genres of art and architecture/housing may be identified, traditional and contemporary forms.[2]

Neither of these categories constitutes a completely isolated study or a balanced chronological narrative. Although the timeless precolonial trends have been retained, they are gradually adapting to the postcolonial styles and tastes and the use of modern tools and technology. With the exception of buildings, quarters, and infrastructures associated with modern institutions and businesses, the architectural landscape has retained much of its precolonial identity. French colonialism beginning in the twentieth century introduced painting as a separate art form; however, Western-style painting is yet to assume a distinct Moroccan image. It still exists as one of those indulgences of the eccentric and rich with a taste for Western lifestyles. The traditional artisans and craftsmen have continued to dominate, using modern technology to standardize their products for both the local and international markets.

ART

Traditional Art Forms

Morocco's hybrid artistic tradition is an important part of its architecture and housing. Decorative art forms consist of patterns produced on stone, fabric, earth, ceramics, plaster, wood, and tile. Elaborate tile mosaics (or ceramic tiles) called *zelliges* are a striking form of traditional art of Morocco. The most visible success of this art is best observed with the decoration of mosques, palaces, colleges, and other public buildings, including private homes of affluent individuals. *Zelliges* are arranged in different patterns and colors. Some experts have observed that the most distinctive aspect of Moroccan architecture is the recurring form of the horseshoe arch (structured round and/or pointed), which actually is one of the legacies bequeathed to North Africa via Spain by the Visigoths of Scandinavia. In Morocco, the horseshoe arches are an integral part of framing and decoration of gateways, doors, and windows of any sizable building. A detailed study of this form of artistic style observes that "decoration is so much a part of architecture that a building is as much the creation of the specialized craftsmen who adorned it with plasters, wood, mosaic, and tile as of the masons who outlined the basic structures."[3]

Although elaborate artistic decorations are usually a component of architecture, this is not necessarily a rule for the Berbers of southern Morocco, where the buildings are not always decorated. This exception is partly connected with the use of certain building materials such as pressed earth and

Palace mosaic, Meknes. Courtesy of Valerie Orlando.

straw, which are not easily amenable to elaborate decorative patterns. Here, the mental disposition toward architecture is determined first and foremost by the search for security. This explains the location in the precolonial era of most houses on hilltops, ridges, and bluffs.

Besides crafts employed in architectural decorations, a rich harvest of locally produced handicrafts are made by specialized and talented Moroccans with the skills to produce items for fashion and household use in forms of stone, silver and gold, fabric, leather and skin, wood, earthenware or ceramics, and iron and brass. Among other handcrafts, Moroccan leather, pottery, brass trays, and iron grillwork are particularly recognized internationally for their finesse. Stone carving is one of the indigenous artworks of Morocco. The "desert rose" of the Sahara is a typical stone with a crystal formation that makes a fine decorative object. Soapstone, a soft local stone, is amenable to carving items like animal and human figurines. Other artworks in stone are paperweights, candleholders, and boxes.

In Morocco, smithing is a traditional art that goes far back in time. Moroccan silversmiths, for instance, are exceptional because they fashion their jewelry by first removing the silver from the ore. Silver jewelry comes in different forms, but the most fashionable among Moroccan women appears to be the heavy solid silver bracelets with deeply engraved patterns. Other items include earrings, anklets, and necklaces. Some of these are elaborately fashioned with semiprecious stones or studs with the surface polished to a high shine. Similarly, gold jewelry is an important and unique part of the smithing industry.

Gold jewelry is mainly found in the big cities, where the rich merchants, government officials, and other wealthy individuals and visitors are most likely to patronize the jewelers.

One distinctive souvenir from Fès is known as the *hzam,* which is entirely different from the gorgeous and expensive silk belts also known by the same name in Fès. This *hzam* is often used for picture framing and embroidered with modern patterns. A *hzam* measures about four centimeters wide by two or four meters long. Another souvenir is the *mdemma,* which is a waist belt made of superior leather and fixed with satin strips and gold embroidery. It comes with a highly ornamental buckle made of gold or silver. In Morocco, goldsmiths usually have their own separate quarters where security is provided and members of the guilds operate with utmost discretion.

Weaving is one of Morocco's oldest traditions and crafts. Weavers use wool, silk, and cotton to produce an assortment of products such as long robes, tablecloths, blankets, and tea set covers in both plain and colorful patterns. Another common form of weaving in Morocco is basketry. Moroccan artisans use canes to produce assortments of items of different shapes and sizes for decorative and household purposes. Some baskets are designed with covers for storage; others are produced as toys of different sizes and shapes. The most popular products made by weavers are well-designed and beautiful oriental rugs, which are commonly used for wall decorations and floor coverings and covers for cushions, beds, pillows, chairs, and other items of furniture. The exquisite silk and cotton throws of Morocco come in different bright patterns and colors. Some types of rugs are used for special occasions such as weddings.

There are wide-ranging regional variations in Moroccan arts and crafts. For instance, the rugs produced in the country are of different qualities, patterns, and colors, and they are usually named after their specific villages, towns, or cities of origin. Rugs made in big cities such as Fès, Casablanca, Tangier, and Rabat are named after their cities of origin. These are also identified as "city rugs" because of their characteristic bright colors and rectangular patterns. Rabat, the city capital, is renowned for producing one of the finest oriental rugs, which is also among the most expensive in the world. Those originating from the dominantly Berber homelands of the High Atlas are generally identified by their more original patterns. According to one source, "rugs of the High Atlas type have a rustic weave with large knots, with four or five shoots of weft between each row of knots. The depth of the pile is intended to compensate for the low number of knots. The Lozenge pattern completely covers the field."[4] These rugs are predominantly brown with golden yellow borders. They are ideal for modern or rustic interior designs.

Similarly, artisans in Morocco have been successful in producing thousands of products made from leather and skin. The abundance of sheep and goats raised in the country provides a rich source of leather and skin from which a wide variety of products such as luggage, satchels, belts, wallets, musical instruments, slippers, and shoes are made. Desk sets and office furnishings with arabesque designs are also made from leather and skin both for the local and international markets. Among the various types of handbags is a small type especially made to carry the Muslim holy book, the Quran. The more fashionable ones are made of durable sheepskin finished with colorfully embroidered designs and provided with shoulder straps and zippers. Moroccan leather fashion products, like their rugs, rank among the most renowned in the world. For instance, the traditional slippers (*bulgha* or *baboosh*), which have been improved upon with the aid of modern tools and technology and produced in different colors, sizes, and patterns, have today found their ways into the bedrooms of Belgians, Britons, and French.

Woodworking is another important part of art design and decoration in Morocco. Skillful artists have successfully used wood indigenous to Morocco for various products. For instance, in Marrakech and the rocky city of Azrou, lying south of Meknès (in Berber *azrou* means "rock"), the woodworkers and cabinetmakers mostly use hardwoods that grow in the local forests, including cedar, pine, olive, and walnut. Cedar is also used in making coffers, or strongboxes, specially constructed to hold important

Store in Meknes displaying an array of exquisite oriental rugs. Courtesy of Valerie Orlando.

items such as money, jewelry, and, traditionally, women's caftans. Among other woods, ebony (a hardwood that grows in the tropics) and citrus are ideal for products that require a delicate surface finish, such as chessboards. Thyua is a wood often preferred for furniture, including marquetry coffee tables and decorated caskets. It is also used for making hard-carved boxes for jewelry and for sizable cigarette cases that one can easily carry. Crafts-men working in different kinds of wood also produce large trays that appear to be woven like a carpet. Intricately painted wood is also very popular in Morocco. The old city of Fès is particularly known for its wooden cribs that have a brightly painted finish.

Pottery is another traditional form of Moroccan art. Potters working with clay and burnt earth design pots, kettles, and vases of different shapes and sizes for household, decorative, and musical purposes. Other items com-monly produced by potters include plates, jugs, coffee-sets, saucers, cups, and cooking pots glazed with black designs. Some ceramic products are covered with fine leather and decorated with gold design. Safi (or Asfi), a seaport city of western Morocco that lies on the coastal plains along the Atlantic Ocean, is widely acknowledged as the pottery capital of the world. Safi potters are also proficient in metalwork.

Metal and brass work are found in a wide variety of protective, artistic, and decorative grilles as well as household items such as lamps, candleholders, small tables, chairs, and various kinds of ornamented items. Brass work is an important part of the handicraft industry. Artistically decorated candleholders, trays, and ashtrays are produced in brass. Some of the trays are big enough to be placed on wrought iron legs to make a table. Other products include finely carved door knockers, sugar boxes, incense burners, and lanterns. Some Moroccan lanterns feature sapphire, ruby, emerald, amethyst, and topaz colored glass that cast a charming light. The most popular lamp is made from leather colored with henna decorations.

To preserve their rich artistic tradition, postcolonial governments in Morocco have stimulated interest in the growth and development of handi-crafts by encouraging skilled craftsmen to use the various art centers estab-lished across the country. Every year, the pool of artisans and craftsmen who participate in the annual Month of Handicrafts festivals are recognized for their contribution toward the preservation of the indigenous culture. The most outstanding artworks presented at the festivals are reserved for display in the various national and regional museums in Rabat, Tangier, Marrakech, Fès, and Meknès. Although local artisans have continued to dominate the industry with indigenous crafts and items produced with local materials for commercial purposes, Western-style painting has yet to win a popular audience in Morocco.

As a distinct art form, contemporary painting remains the prerogative of the educated elite or the so-called Westernized individuals. Most Moroccan painters were trained in France just like many of their patrons, who have had some kind of connection with Europe and other Western countries, including the United States and Canada. Contemporary Moroccan painters primarily use natural subjects such as the human form, trees, street scenes, animals, and other objects in their natural habitats. These works are mostly produced in Western-style abstractions. Generally, Islam prohibits the depiction of any living thing that has a soul, including people and animals.

Moroccan artists capture the people's worldview, their ideas of creation, individual and common aspirations, value systems, family connections, social life, history, politics, and trade and occupations. Art objects exchanged between rulers of different countries serve as *objets d'envoi*.[5] Artistic work in Morocco also provides information on processes through which society has adapted to sociopolitical and economic changes from one historical era to another. A closer study of art forms may reveal regional variations as well as origins and patterns of dispersion of a material culture. In precolonial Africa, artists were widely revered for their special skills rather than for their wealth. As culture carriers, they also help to preserve their local history by providing representations of battles and warriors, dances and performers, manners of dressing, visitors, heroes, kings, queens, and other important personalities. In modern Morocco, the prominent role played by artisans in promoting the tourist industry has brought them both popularity and prosperity. Although the local artist in the past did not get much monetary reward, his skill was nonetheless widely respected and appreciated far beyond his land. Similarly, successful contemporary artists have also carved out a niche for themselves.

Contemporary Art Forms

With the dawn of European colonialism in 1912, artistic expression began its gradual transition to what is today referred to as contemporary. The French colonial schools, established after the protectorate agreement of 1912, introduced young Moroccans to the French ways of life and European art. Moroccans who continued their studies in France and other parts of Europe specialized in art as an academic discipline in the hope of expanding the rich artistic heritage of Morocco with new ideas, expressions, and media learned from the West. The Western-educated artists, who are often affiliated with an institution of higher learning, constitute the majority of the producers of the so-called contemporary or modern arts. The art studios and business ideas of the contemporary artists have been fashioned after their foreign models. Among them are Andre Elbaz, a Moroccan Jew, whose works depict such images from Jewish spiritual culture as the city of Jerusalem, the prayer, typical synagogue settings, and the Holocaust.[6] Although Elbaz and others such as Ben Haim paint in the abstract expressionist tradition, their choice of themes also reflects their multicultural indigenous environment.

With the strong reputation of Moroccan traditional art and architecture worldwide, contemporary artists are confronted with daunting challenges in breaking new ground. To win recognition and respect, contemporary artists must improve on existing legacies. Considering the excellent craftsmanship that has flourished in Morocco since the sixteenth century, the contemporary artist can tap from both traditional and European art forms to create something innovative. A good example along this line is the Wafabank art gallery in Casablanca. In 1988, Wafabank, a major commercial financial institution in Morocco, displayed modern art in the foyer of its corporate headquarters. Through its patronage of local art, the bank solidified its image as part of a Moroccan nation. While promoting an image of the investment institution, the bank also tried to project its image as a competitive participant in global capitalism. The artistic imagery represented modern Morocco turned toward the future.[7]

Meanwhile, existing religious and traditional values tend to constrain the freedom of painters to explore their talents. In Islam, certain kinds of artistic expression are not permitted. Muslims hold the belief that angels will not enter a house that has pictures or sculptures of anything that contains a soul. For the artist, this taboo is even more restrictive in view of the competition from Western counterparts who are free of religious, social, or political constraints. Consequently, the contemporary Moroccan painter is trapped between two worlds—religious strictures and secular enchantments. The path to artistic success lies in making the best out of this dualism.

Because of religious restrictions, European artists who visited Morocco in the colonial period usually stayed in the Jewish quarters, or *mellahs* (a common word for the various Jewish quarters of Moroccan towns and cities). The *mellahs* were more accessible to Europeans than the old Muslim quarters known as old medina. While the European artists introduced Moroccan Jews to Western paintings, European painters were in turn influenced by Jewish culture and, by extension, Moroccan art forms. The paintings of the Europeans and their Moroccan cohorts depicted Jewish social ceremonies such as weddings. Images of Jewish women featured prominently in both the painting and the photography of visiting European artists. This was because Jewish women were more likely to be comfortable posing for the artists.

ARCHITECTURE

Traditional Architecture/Housing

Moroccan architecture has been heavily impacted by Islamic traditions and later European influences, the climate, modes of religious worship and rituals, regional histories, and local materials. All have combined to give Moroccan architecture a diverse but unique expression. Westerners refer to Morocco's architectural style as Hispano-Moorish because of the influence brought by the Arabs who were expelled from Europe in the eighth century. The styles and patterns brought from Spain by these Arabs soon expanded, emerging as a popular culture. Hispano-Moorish architecture peaked in Morocco between the twelfth and fourteenth centuries, with the horseshoe-shaped arch emerging as the most distinctive feature of the style.

This form of traditional architecture is best appreciated in the exquisite mosques and temples that dot the large cities in Morocco. The medieval architectural landmarks found everywhere are eloquent reminders about the people's diverse cultural heritage, style and taste, politics, ethnic and religious identity, and the way Muslims, Jews, and foreigners lived and interacted with one another. The Muslim medinas, the Jewish *mellahs,* the fortresses of the Berbers and their Marabout saints, the palaces of the sultans, and the Casbahs of the provincial and local governors (viziers) and the local judges *(qaids)* all

Medieval Castle in Ouarzazate, Morocco. Courtesy of Valerie Orlando.

reflect important parts of this history. Each ethnic group in a particular city has its own quarter. This reminds historians about authority and power relations, social customs, ethnic and religious identities, and patterns of civic engagements.[8]

Today, the inner parts of the Atlas Mountains and the southern fringes of the desert remain as predominantly Berber homelands. The Berbers have, with some modifications, retained the fortresslike forms of architecture known as the Casbah. It is typically constructed to withstand enemy assault. In essence, a Casbah in the Berber country is a feudal castle or a fortified village with interconnected parts. In the era of the Islamic invasions of North Africa and Spain, a fortified section of the Casbah known as the *ksar* was where loyal residents sought protection in times of danger. In the Sahara and Atlas Mountain regions, however, the word *ksar* generally refers to fortified and walled villages.[9] The Casbahs also serve as both residential houses and storerooms.

Some of the houses built before the 1920s were located about 300 meters from one another and planned without windows. They have towers and pillboxes from which a family could repel enemy attacks. Others have only a few openings with sides opening outward, usually for allowing the firing of cannon. Although there are few dangers for residents today, some authorities have noted the resilience of "the architectonic notion of a house as a defensive fortress against a dangerous external world continues, as each house is surrounded

Medieval castle in Essaouira, Morocco. Courtesy of Valerie Orlando.

by groves of prickly pears and inhospitable domestic dogs."[10] Also, the camps of the black, squat, and goat-hair tents of the Berber nomads still exist in the isolated mountain steppes bordering the Sahara.[11]

Big cities such as Tangier, Fès, Rabat, and Casablanca have landmarks that define Morocco's artistic and architectural achievements in more elaborate, diverse, and cosmopolitan settings. Tangier, for instance, reflects a multicultural foundation of the people's architecture. The architecture of the city tells a part of the people's history. Tangier has five-star hotels, which are primarily Muslim public buildings rebuilt to attract tourists and other visitors. This trend in remodeling, which began with the Mohammed V mausoleum and a set of other large projects, has been branded by some scholars as the "Hassanian architectural style."[12] Tangier also hosts Chaouen, the palace of the sharifs—that is, the descendants of the Prophet Muhammad. Another important historical structure of the city is Abdel el Krim's well-secured fortress, which tells a history of the fierce Berber anticolonial resistance in Morocco from 1912 to 1934. This castle is now a popular tourist attraction. Overall, the most impressive architectural landmark of Tangier is the twelfth-century medina with its 27 mosques and markets and its shops (souks) that sell crafts to tourists.

Typical fortified desert home in the Errachidean Tafilalet region between the Atlas Mountains to the north and the Sahara to the south. Courtesy of Valerie Orlando.

Fès, popularly known as the Three Cities, including the adjacent suburbs of Moulay-Idriss and the ancient Roman city of Volubilis to the west, represents an important part of the architectural history of Morocco. Besides being the third largest city in Morocco, Fès is generally known in the Arab world for its wonderful marble temples, sculptures, luxurious baths, and mosaic floors. The walled section of its medina (or Arab quarter), located on a hill to the east, remains as one of the most complex architectural landmarks of the town. Some of the historical landmarks include ancient monuments, mosques, Quranic colleges, inns, *mellahs,* and shops. The medina (also called Fès el Bali) is in the style of a Roman amphitheater. Directly facing the main city gates is a hillside studded with stones of ancient cemeteries, and nearby are the larger tombs of the revered righteous men (*Wali Saleh*) of Fès. The streets are typically narrow with a network of alleyways that were not originally meant for modern cars. The houses are often tall. Also in the medina section of Fès is the Dar Batha, a nineteenth-century palace now serving as the Museum of Moroccan Art and Handicrafts. Another important landmark is the Bou Imania Medersa, a fourteenth-century college complex, which represents a fine example of Merinid architecture. The walls are covered with mosaics, carved plaster, and elaborately patterned cut and uncut loops. Its penthouse is finished with details(e.g. elaborate artistic decorations and paintings), and the courtyard is paved in romantic colors.

Most traditional buildings in Morocco are modeled after the mosques, thereby capturing the dominant religion of the people. The mosques are typically constructed with a high entrance door and a green tiled roof. The courtyards have a fountain for ritual ablution, and a hall is divided into aisles to separate the sexes. A recess in the wall (mihrab) is strategically placed to show the direction of Mecca. All the mosques have a pulpit from which the prayer leader (Imam) officiates during Friday congregational prayers.

The Quranic colleges and universities established early in the twelfth century were closely modeled after the mosques, with courtyards that have fountains and with prayer halls. The structures are also decorated with mosaic tiles, glasswork, stucco, and Kufic script (named after the Iraqi town of Kufa where this form of art originated).

Fès also has the oldest and largest Jewish quarter *(mellah)* in Morocco, established in 1438.[13] Although the *mellahs* of Morocco, including the one in Fès, are now mostly deserted, they provide information on Jewish social life in Morocco. In this part of the Muslim world, walls characteristically surrounded each *mellah,* especially those built in the period of religious fanaticism under the Almohad dynasty (c. 1062–1269). The *mellah* of Fès was built by Sultan Abu Said (died 1250) and was located close to his palace to ensure the protection of the Jews from Muslim fanatics. A recent study of Jewish

Fez, the most precious of all Moroccan cities and one of the most important places in the Islamic world. Courtesy of Valerie Orlando.

mellahs in Marrakech, by an art historian at the Hebrew University Jerusalem, reports that the houses followed a rudimentary style, which extended to other structures in the quarters across Morocco, including Fès. All the synagogues were built virtually in the same pattern across Morocco. They were typically located in a narrow alley. The slightly irregular red clay walls had "an unfinished quality to them like the huts niched in the slopes that blend into the landscape of southern Morocco."[14]

Even though a mass exodus of Moroccan Jews occurred in the wake of the Arab-Israeli conflicts beginning with the founding of the state of Israel in 1948, most of the synagogues are still standing in the *mellahs,* even though the quarters are now largely occupied by Muslims. A characteristic feature of the synagogues is an unmarked entrance located off a dim alley that leads through a door to a rectangular room *(ezrat nashim)* reserved for women. This provision for women is apparently a twentieth-century innovation in Morocco. In the past, women were traditionally restricted to the entrance of a synagogue. The small rooms of a synagogue were constructed in a row, with a window in the ceiling as the only source of light. Inside the synagogue, the Ark of Covenant, symbolizing God's special covenant with the Jews, is usually located against an eastern wall, facing the direction of Jerusalem. The lectern, originally made of wood, is positioned at the center of the western wall of the synagogue. Newer lecterns in Jewish synagogues, like that of "Alzama" (one of a series of newly designed

House in the Medina, Fez. Courtesy of Valerie Orlando.

Interior garden of a house in the old medina section of Fez. Courtesy of Valerie Orlando.

synagogues built around a large and well-maintained courtyard), constructed in the early twentieth century in Marrakech, are made of marble. Red clay benches covered with colored fabric and small cushions line the sides. In the center of the synagogue—that is between the lectern and the Ark—is a row of wooden chairs. A common characteristic of all Moroccan synagogues is the

Interior of a medina house, Fez. Courtesy of Valerie Orlando.

abundance of oil lamps *(qandils)* lit in memory of the dead. The *qandil* is suspended by chains and ends in a silver or copper ring in which the lamp is set. The wick has been replaced in many lamps by electric bulbs. Whereas some synagogues are smaller and more modest, others, like some found in Fès and Meknès, are elaborately ornamented. For instance, the Sadoun synagogue in Fès is one of the most lavish in Morocco. Its walls are completely covered in fine plaster and ornamentation with tilted glass panes in the windows above them. This building demonstrates the pervading impact of Muslim traditions, which extends not only to mosques but also to other public buildings such as palaces and houses decorated in stucco and ceramic tiles *(zelliges)*. In other words, Jewish synagogues were constructed on the same pattern as other building, and their artistic decorations have been influenced by Berber, Islamic, and European cultures. Synagogues build by Moroccan Jews and recent immigrants depict regional diversities and traditions that are impossible to assign to a single culture.

A discussion about the history of architecture and housing in Fès would be incomplete without a brief look at Moulay-Idriss—a suburb lying to the west of Fès and named after the founder of Morocco's first dynasty. The town has a mausoleum *(dareeh)* containing the remains of the respected Moulay Idriss I. Because it is a sacred center, Sufis (a sect in North African Islam) mostly inhabit the area. Tourists are allowed to visit but are prohibited to spend the night here. Housing and architecture in Moulay-Idriss represent primarily the original

Muslim style. Narrow, windowless lanes, decorated with lovely carvings on square cedar doors, lead up to the Casbah. In the rich neighborhoods, the entrance doors were constructed to ensure the privacy of the occupants.

As one of the legacies bequeathed by the Merinidian (c. 1248–1420) era sultans who first established their capital here in the mid-thirteenth century, the town is lined with such splendid structures as Muslim colleges, libraries, and the sultans' palaces.[15] The interior decorations of the buildings were specifically designed. The ceiling arches are skillfully carved cedar. The finish work reveals much about the Moroccans reputation in stuccowork. The marble, mosaics, earthenware tiles, and marked enamel plates are all outstanding. The doors are finished with gilded leather and the portals studded with chased bronze sheets. By the time of the Almohad dynasty, Fès had about

> 785 mosques and other places of devotion, nearly 100,000 houses, 81 fountains and 93 public baths and 476 caravansaries and fondouk rest-houses.... The historical picture of the city is rounded off as we learn that it then had 3,064 weaving-mills, 116 dyeworks, 168 pottery establishments and 86 tanneries, while in the Fès souks there were fewer than 9,183 shops in which the famous products of North Africa's most accomplished craftsmen were on sale.[16]

Although a complete account of art and architecture in all the cities and towns of Morocco is impossible here, Morocco's capital, Rabat, and Casablanca,

Historic village of Moulay Idris. Courtesy of Valerie Orlando.

the third largest city in Africa after Lagos (Nigeria) and Cairo (Egypt), will be covered briefly. Rabat was founded in the twelfth century. Today it is a cosmopolitan capital city of gardens *(riyadhs)* and monumental structures. The medina section of Rabat, built in the seventeenth century, still retains its Andalusian character because it housed Muslims originally driven from Spain. Fortified walls surround the historic Quadias fortress, which is accessible through a gateway built during the reign of Yacoub (or Jacob) El Mansour (1185–1195). The main gate leads into the inner garden, designed in 1915. Bougainvillea covers the wall, and birds build nests on the barricades. Installed in the gardens of Casbah is a smaller palace that now serves as the museum of Oudaia. The building was originally built in the seventeenth century. The ceremonial hall is adorned with the best oriental rugs made in Rabat. The terrace has a pond. Inside are a set of local musical instruments and an exhibition hall for jewelry. Another salon is completed with a brocaded divan, a copper incense burner, sculptured chests, and embroidered cushions. This section is reserved for rituals and customs. Like every other city, Rabat also has a Jewish quarter *(mellah)*. One of the most prominent features of the city is the imposing royal palace, where the king resides with his family and where he meets with state officials, friends, important dignitaries, and foreign envoys.

All the royal palaces in Morocco were designed with the help of top artists and craftsmen in the kingdom. They demonstrate the power and authority of the king as the father and custodian of the nation. Most of the king's palaces in Morocco have very plain exteriors. Like the mosques and Islamic colleges, the palace courtyard is the central feature, and rooms are constructed around it. The judgment hall is finished with an elaborate and spacious balcony from which the sultan receives homage from his subjects.

Casablanca, the "white city," is the most "modern" of all the cities in Morocco and has more Western-style structures than the other cities. The city is particularly distinguished for its wide streets, in contrast with the narrow streets of old cities like Fès and Tangier. Like the other cities, however, Casablanca still has its original Arab settlement, or "old medina," with its narrow streets with weathered houses. There are also magnificent mosques built during the reign of Sidi Mohammed be Abdella (1757–1790).

As a modern city, Casablanca is unique for its new residential and business quarters—called "new medina" *(villes nouvelles)*. The French established the *villes nouvelles* in 1921 as part of the innovation that brought colonialism to the people. New medina is home to Mohammed V's (died 1961) magnificent palace, erected at the end of World War I in 1919, which remains as one of the city's principal monuments. Government and private businesses, however, have erected several Western-style high-rise buildings. Among these, the most impressive is perhaps the United Nations Square, which is completed with a post office, municipal theater, and city hall, along with a McDonald's. Also, both the Arab League headquarters and the imposing French government's building (Place de France) stand out. The emerging Western-style architecture is fast encroaching on the seemingly unyielding Oriental tradition. The residential areas are complete with gardens, Moorish fountains, amusement parks, golf courses, and colonial houses.

This picture of affluence is in sharp contrast to the surrounding slums *(bidonvilles),* which first appeared in Casablanca in the 1920s after the expansion of the population of the city. The *bidonvilles* often serve as transit stations for newly arrived families who can find affordable accommodations in the makeshift structures formerly occupied by renters who moved to the city after securing better-paying jobs. The government in Morocco has, within its limited ability, tried to provide a suitable accommodation for its citizens, but this has been constrained by lack of adequate resources in the face of a fast-growing population.

Overall, architecture and housing in Casablanca, Rabat, Fès, Tangier, and other Moroccan cities "stand in sharp contrast with a Western discourse that visualizes the Moroccan city as disordered, its streets insalubrious, its water system in a state of dilapidation."[17] It is important to reiterate that contemporary housing and architecture in Morocco are undergoing a dynamic and ongoing process. This will continue to adjust and expand in response to both local and international adaptations in style, taste, and technology. It is also crucial to note that ethnic, class, and urban and rural differences have combined in different degrees in determining the direction of the recent developments. The new generation of technocrats and young people in the big cities are predisposed to Western-style residential houses. The poorer individuals who cannot afford accommodation in the palatial neighborhoods are forced to make do with shanties or the older and more traditional architectural styles. Against the notion that tends to see Islamic architecture as relatively static, one must emphasize that it, as in every culture, is dynamic in nature.

NOTES

1. A similar point has been made by Wilhelmina Schripper in "The Verbal and the Visual in a Globalizing Context: African and European Connections as an Ongoing Process," *Research in African Literature* 31, no. 4 (2000): 139–54.

2. See also Bogumil Jewsiewicki, *Cheri Samba: The Hybridity of Art* [*L' hybridité d' un art*] (Westmount, Quebec: Galerie Amrad African Art Publications, 1995).

3. Richard F. Nyrop et al., *Area Handbook for Morocco* (Washington, D.C.: U.S. Government Printing Office, 1972), 139.

4. E. Gans-Ruedin, *The Connoisseur's Guide to Oriental Carpets,* trans. Valerie Howard (Rutland, VT: Charles E. Tuttle, 1971), 417.

5. For a good discussion on this, see Christine Mullen and Sarah Fez, eds., *Objects as Envoys: Cloth, Imagery, and Diplomacy in Madagascar* (Washington, D.C.: Smithsonian Institution, National Museum of African Art in association with the University of Washington Press, 2002), 1.

6. See also Daniel J. Schroeter and Vivian B. Mann, eds., *Morocco: Jews and Art in a Muslim Land* (London: Merrell, 2000).

7. James McDougall, ed., *Nation, Society and Culture in North Africa* (Portland, OR: Frank Cass, 2003), 136, 144. See also Katarzyna Pieprzak, "Citizens and Subjects in the Bank: Corporate Visions of Modern Art and Moroccan Identity," *Journal of North African Studies* 8, no. 1 (2003): 131–54.

8. A historian of African architecture has also underscored this point in a recent book; see Nnamdi Elleh, *Architecture and Power in Africa* (Westport, CT: Praeger, 2002), 112.

9. Hsain Illahiane, "The Break-up of the Ksar: Changing Settlement Patterns and Environmental Management in Southern Morocco," *Africa Today* 48, no. 1 (2001): 21–48.

10. Roger Joseph and Terri Brint Joseph, *The Rose and the Thorn: Semiotic Structures in Morocco* (Tucson: University of Arizona Press, 1987), 16.

11. Hans Seligo, *Morocco,* trans. G. A. Colville (Garden City, NY: Doubleday, 1966), 49.

12. Philippe Ploquin and Mohammed-Allal Sinaceur, *La Mosquée Hassan II* [*The Hassan II Mosque*] (Dremil-Lafage, France: Editions D. Briand, 1993), 17.

13. The oldest of all the Jewish *mellahs* in Morocco is the Fez el-Bali (the "old city") founded by Idriss II in the ninth century.

14. Ariella Amar, "Moroccan Synagogues: A Survey," *The Israeli Review of Arts and Letters* 106 (February 1999): 1–6. For a detailed study of Jewish life in Morocco, see the impressive study by Daniel J. Schroeter, *The Sultan's Jew: Morocco and the Sephardi World* (Stanford, CA: Stanford University Press, 2002).

15. Seligo, *Morocco,* 11.

16. Ibid., 11–12.

17. Susan Gilson Miller, "Watering the Garden of Tangier: Colonial Contestations in a Moroccan City," in Susan Slyomovics, ed., *The Walled Arab City in Literature, Architecture and History: The Living Medina in the Maghrib* (Portland, OR: Frank Cass, 2001), 42.

5

Cuisine and Traditional Dress

CUISINE

MOROCCAN CUISINE AND EATING habits are expressive forms of sociocultural practices that denote personal, familial, and social habits and identities. They also underscore societal values and etiquette because the preparation of certain foods and dishes are dictated by customs and rules at certain periods of the day or year. Over the centuries, the natural gifts of ocean, sea, and arable parts of Morocco's diverse land have enabled the growth of a wide variety of fruits, meat, vegetables, and seafood that support the population and enrich the people's diets. Even regions threatened by drought *(dhamurth nj-bur)* such as some parts of the Rif Mountains, as opposed to the irrigated *(dhamurth w-aman)* parts, have continued to sustain life with the success of barley cultivation as well as poultry, sheep, and goat farms.

Strategically located at one of the most important termini of ancient trading circuits, Morocco's kitchen today is an amalgam of different cultures. The "kitchen of Morocco combines European infusion, Arab trade and age-old custom."[1] The Arabs, who appeared in Morocco in the late seventh century, brought with them via the trans-Saharan and trans-Mediterranean trade routes new recipes, varieties of breads, and spices from China, India, Malaysia, and West Africa. From the Ottomans, grilling and barbecue were popularized. From the Portuguese and Spanish, the Moroccans learned new dishes and received food crops such as maize from the New World in the fifteenth century. Under colonial rule between 1912 and 1956, the French introduced pastries, desserts, ice creams, confectionaries, and the custom of mixing grilled food with salads with lettuce and so on. The French also introduced new techniques of agriculture, which have improved crop yield, expanded the vineyards, and improved the quality and quantity of wine in Morocco. However, most of the cooking methods, cuisine, dietary habits, and social customs that exist today have long been part of the indigenous Berber culture before the various alien influences made inroads. Others are practices common to Africans, Asians, Arabs, and Europeans. This diversity forms a gastronomy that reflects a vibrant and lively culture explored by the women *(dada)* and professional chefs of the country and is what is now popularly acknowledged as Moroccan cuisine.

Popular Cuisine

In a book written for an American audience, Paula Wolfert, a former resident of Morocco, identified four dishes that she claimed to be the most popular among Moroccans. Top among these is couscous, which is a type of grain processed from semolina. Couscous can also be made from grains such as barley, millet, and cornmeal. The next in popularity, according to the author, is a huge pie or thick pastry called *bisteeya* (also *b'steeya, bastela, bastila,* and *pastilla*). Then there is the mouthwatering roasted lamb *(mechoui* or *mashw)* prepared as barbeque. The fourth is a chicken dish *(djej emshmel)* prepared with lemon and olives.[2] Although this list may still be relevant, it is difficult to choose only four from the numerous dishes of Morocco. First, Moroccan cuisine is dynamic, as the women and professional cooks continue to experiment with a wide range of recipes. Second, as people often say, "the best meals are not found in restaurants" but in the home. It is therefore hard to make any conclusive statement from restaurant meals. Food culture differs from person to person, family to family, and region to region. Moreover, the foodstuffs available to the rich are not the same ones that are accessible to the poor. Simple meals made from wheat or barley are the most affordable for the average person in Morocco. Third, a survey of Morocco's popular cuisine must include a discussion of bread. Among other significances, bread is not only a common part of everyday meals but is also perceived as a sacred gift from Allah (God).

*Bread (*Ksra *or* Khboz*)*

A common Moroccan proverb challenges the deprived to "manage with bread and butter until God sends the honey." This adage emphasizes both the availability of bread to everybody, rich or poor, and its reverence as a sacred food. The Berbers of the Rif Mountains have long sustained themselves with their staple breads made from barley. They supplement their favorite breads with a variety of other products such as potatoes, tomatoes, onions, garlic, pepper, squash, fruits, and nuts. Berber men cultivate barley, which their women produce into flour and then bake it into bread. In fact, the imagery of converting barley to bread "is very clearly recognized in the [traditional] wedding ceremony, when the bride brings barley seed to her husband's house to scatter in the coming cycle of planting."[3]

Until the late 1980s, almost all households in Morocco would bake their own bread. The development of modern cities and the increasing demand of professional careers on family life are beginning to change this practice. Originally, community ovens (known as *fran*) were strategically located in every neighborhood to enable families to bake their bread. This was before families started buying their own ovens. In the public bakeries, each family distinguished their breads with identification signs and letters. With the increasing demands of urban life, professional careers, and women's gradual departure from the traditional role of a housewife, some individuals and families have little time to make their own breads.

Moroccans bake a wide variety of breads from coarse barley, flour, wheat, sorghum, and millet. Often the bread is thin, flat, and round or shaped into a long crispy dough. Women knead the dough methodically until the yeast is evenly distributed and enriched with herbs, spices, protein, and other ingredients. The Berber women are famous for a special kind of local bread called *therfist,* which is unleavened bread prepared in sheets. The Tuaregs of the southern part of the country bake on hot sand and call their special bread *tagella.* Typical Moroccan breads include *khboz bishemar* and *khboz milka.* The latter is flattened circular dough cooked until brown on both sides. The *khboz bishemar* is baked in a unique form with fat and spices stuffed inside the dough. As it bakes, the fat runs out through holes pierced in the dough, leaving behind a mouthwatering aroma of spices and herbs. Holiday bread is originally from the port city of Essaouira on the Atlantic west coast of Marrakech. It is prepared according to special family recipes with dry yeast, sweet butter, granulated sugar *(sukkar),* salt, sesame seeds, cornmeal, aniseed, and buttermilk. Generally, Moroccan breads are heavy, spicy, soft-crusted, highly absorbent, and ideal for dipping into the special stew, *tajine.* In a society where most people eat with their fingers, bread often serves as a utensil for stirring and bringing food into the mouth. It is a custom in Morocco for one person to distribute bread when all are seated at the table.[4]

Couscous (Grain)

Couscous is widely acknowledged as the national dish of Morocco, and it is also popular in the whole of the Maghreb. It is of Berber origin, and it means more than the prepared dish and the granules of semolina. Couscous also means "food" in Moroccan Arabic because it is generally affordable to the poor and therefore a regular part of the people's daily meals. According to a study made in 1972, most families were still sending their "wheat to the local mill to be ground to the degree of fineness they preferred."[5] Couscous may also be prepared with other types of grains, including wheat, barley, sprouts, corn, millet, crushed acorns, and even breadcrumbs. Although the various grains can be prepared in dissimilar ways, they turn into couscous only when covered and cooked over low heat and allowed to simmer. Steaming is said to be a traditional Berber way of cooking because of the scarcity of wood in the semiarid land. Couscous may be served with stew *(tajine)* with different types of meats and vegetables such as turnips, chickpeas, and onions. In Fès, the stew is often light, and the ingredients are delicately cooked and seasoned with onions, black pepper, saffron, and ginger. It is normal to serve couscous with loaves of bread.

The Pastry or Pie (Bisteeya)

Bisteeya is one of the richest and most exotic meals of Morocco. It can be described as a huge pie delicately made of layers of spicy pigeon or chicken, lemony eggs cooked in a savory onion sauce, and toasted and sweetened almonds. Baked together, the recipe forms a uniquely Moroccan pastry. People disagree over the origin of this dish. Some claim it came from Andalusia, Spain, based on the similarity of the word *bisteeya* to the Spanish word *pasteles* (or "pastry confections"). Others postulate that *bisteeya* was brought to Morocco in the seventh century with the invading Arabs from the Middle East and that the Arabs in turn got this recipe from the Chinese. Whatever its origin, the Moroccans, like their Asian, African, and European neighbors, have borrowed and adapted ideas originating from other cultures in creating their distinct ways of life, including food and dietary habits. This pie is typically enormous and must be prepared in a big tray that can serve up to 10 people. The preparation of the dough demands expertise and experience. There are regional variations of *bisteeya.* For instance, in Fès, *bisteeya* is traditionally prepared with pigeon meat (instead of chicken), and the diameter is about 20 or more inches. Pigeons in Morocco are of a different variety from those found in the United States, and so they taste different. The Berbers in the Middle Atlas region of central Morocco make a distinct *bisteeya* with pounded beef or lamb and seasoned with cinnamon and egg. The Berbers call this version of *bisteeya tarkhdoult.* The version made in Marrakech is prepared with milk and orange flower water. Generally, the pastry is prepared according to individual taste.

The Chicken Dish (Djej Emshmel)

The chicken *(djej)* dish is prepared in different ways, but basically it is a lemon and olive stew. As desired, other ingredients, such as eggs and onions, may also be added. The chicken is slowly simmered with olives and preserved lemons in a smooth sauce seasoned with saffron, cumin, ginger, and paprika. When the dish is prepared, as in Meknès, with spiced and creamy lemon and served with olive sauce, it represents the original *djej emshmel.* When the chicken is prepared with a combination of eggs, it becomes *djej masquid bil beid.* When pigeon *(frach)* is substituted for chicken, the dish is called *frach masquid bil beid.* Some families prepare their favorite chicken dish using the locally grown bitter green olives, and the dish is called *djej bil zeetoon meslalla.*

Stew or Sauce (Tajine or Tagine)

The Moroccan traditional stew or *tajine* is of Berber origin and may be prepared in different ways. Actually, the word *tajine,* or *tagine,* is both the name of the completed dish and the name of a locally manufactured pot made from earthenware. The pot comes in different shapes and sizes, and it cooks food slowly. Traditionally, *tajine* is mainly prepared with chicken and lamb. Now it can be prepared with anything, including camel or fish. (What the Moroccans regard as soup [*shourba*] is *harrira,* which is prepared with mutton and spices. *Harrira* is quite different from *tajine.*) The recipe for *tajine* includes heating oil and spices in a cold clay pot. Then the meat or fish is added and cooked over low heat. Finally, vegetables are added and allowed just enough time to cook. The preferred *tajine* is lemon chicken marinated in olive oil, onions, black pepper, salt, saffron, garlic, and mosses.[6]

Spices, Aromatics, and Herbs

The use of spices is perhaps the most distinctive element of Moroccan cuisine. Most of the spices in use today were brought to Morocco many centuries ago from India, China, the Middle East, and sub-Saharan Africa. Given the importance of spices, herbs, and other types of culinary aromatics in Moroccan cuisine, it is propitious to identify some of the most popular spices found there. They are used not only for the enrichment of food flavor and taste but also for their sophisticated medicinal values. The 10 most important spices commonly used are cayenne *(felfla),* cumin *(kamoon),* cinnamon *(karfa),* turmeric *(quekoum),* saffron *(zafrane),* ginger *(skinjbir),* paprika *(felfla hlouwa),* black pepper *(elbezar),* aniseed *(nafaa* or *habbt),* and sesame seeds *(jinjelan).* Other aromatics include allspice *(noioura),* caraway *(karwiya),* cloves *(oud el nouar),* coriander seeds *(kosbour),* gum arabic *(mska),* fenugreek *(helbah),* licorice *(arksous),* honey dates *(nabka),* and orrisroot *(amber el door).* The most popular herbs and plants include onions *(sla),* garlic *(tourma),* parsley *(madnouss),* and green coriander *(kosbour).*[7] The way in which these spices, herbs, and aromatics are used largely depends on individual taste, type of dish, and quantity being prepared.

MEALTIME

In Morocco (unlike the practice in most sub-Saharan African societies where dinner is the major meal of the day), lunch is the main meal and "eat-as-you-can" or "as-you-can-afford" seems to be the common practice. It is only during the month of Ramadan (the month of fasting) that Muslims eat at sunset and before sunrise. Whereas most Africans, especially those in the sub-Saharan region, characteristically serve a single-course meal, Moroccans, like the Europeans, Americans, and Asians, serve several courses. In Morocco there is neither a common national menu to which everybody must adhere nor an established order of serving meals. What is on the menu and how many courses are served depend much on individuals' tastes, family habits, and, more importantly, their financial capacity. A large portion of the foods grown in Morocco is exported to Europe in order for the government and farmers to secure foreign capital for the importation of machines and to finance development projects. Consequently, there is an abnormal problem of food scarcity. The wealthy enjoy sumptuous meals, but the poor rarely eat a balanced diet.

There are three daily meals—breakfast *(futo),* lunch or midday meal *(rada),* and dinner *(asha).* Breakfast is usually light, consisting of bread, butter, olive oil, black olives (dipped in a special salt), jelly, and other simple foods. Bread is the most common food for breakfast. It is eaten with butter or dipped into preserved olive oil with tea and juice.

Lunchtime in Morocco, as in most Mediterranean countries, including modern Spain, is almost inseparable from family and therefore sacred. It is a period of the day for an elaborate family meal as well as a time for rest before returning to work. In line with the law, many businesses and offices are closed for the midday meal, and most family members rush home for lunch. Exceptions include those who work in locations far away from home. With the majority of women still playing the traditional housewife role, the midday meal is elaborate and ritualistic. It therefore offers an ideal setting to assess table manners and eating habits. Lunch preparation may take hours or even days, depending on the type of meal, the size of the family, the number of persons involved in the preparation, and the quality and number of courses planned. Family meals are prepared differently from ceremonial meals. For the women for whom managing the home is their primary duty, cooking is not only a form of expression, it is also a symbol of privilege and power. They begin preparing lunch for their families soon after breakfast is over. In ideal circumstances, the midday meal commences with a series of green vegetables or salads served as appetizers *(tapas).* Stew *(tajine)* or what Americans and other Westerners call soup is served next, with vegetables, hard-boiled eggs, and flat bread. The main dish of the midday meal for well-to-do families is often a lamb or chicken served with a generous measure of couscous, which is also garnished with vegetables.

Considering the typically generous size of the midday meal, dinner is often plain—mainly consisting of the lunch leftovers. Families who can afford them may add salads, omelets, and/or meat. Snacks are not common in the local diet. Rather, varieties of dried fruits and nuts are consumed. Recently, crunchy chips and fast foods have emerged in corner shops across Morocco. This is an aspect of globalization that is increasingly bringing peoples of all cultures into closer contact with Western practices, including tastes for Western food and beverages.[8]

Beverages

The most popular and widely affordable beverages in Morocco include water and mint tea. Also available are wines, coffee, milk, and varieties of fruit drinks. A study has revealed that since World War II when American troops stationed in Morocco introduced Coca-Cola to the people, carbonated mineral waters have found a growing number of consumers.[9] Although ordinary water is cheaper, the privileged are used to drinking water treated with gum arabic (known in Morocco as *mska,* a water-soluble gum obtained from *Acacias arabica* and used in the making of pharmaceuticals, confections, and other products). This is referred to as "perfumed water" because of the sweet-smelling scent and lingering taste of the gum arabic. Across Morocco, obtaining good drinking water can sometimes be a problem, especially in the smaller cities and the semiarid villages of the mountainous countryside. The government has been working to make drinking water available to most parts of the country.

The characteristically sweet mint tea is a national beverage enjoyed in Morocco. British traders brought tea into the country around the first decade of the nineteenth century, and the local people have developed a distinct taste for their special mint tea. The tea may be prepared in different ways, but the basic recipe involves green tea, steeped and laced with a generous amount of white sugar and fresh spearmint. This tea is drunk from small glasses and tastes so sweet that it becomes addictive. Nowadays, the three glassfuls traditionally taken at meals or ceremonies have been more or less abandoned. Those with diabetes or other health concerns must either stay away from it or learn how to drink their tea without sugar.

Moroccans also enjoy wine. The Mediterranean climate is ideal for growing grapes. Initially, Moroccan Jews distilled alcoholic beverages from grapes, dates, honeycombs, pomegranates, and raisins. One of their favorite brews is the fig brandy produced in the Telouet region of the High Atlas Mountains. After the protectorate agreement of 1912, the French established more vineyards across Morocco, especially around Fès, Rabat, and Meknès. These vineyards account for a substantial part of the Maghrebean source that accounts for about 10 percent of world's wine. Moroccan wines include white and red, Cabernet, Sidi Larbi, Vieux Papes, Valpierre, Chaudsoleil, and a special wine called Gris de Boulaouane. Under normal and strict religious observances, Islam abhors the consumption of alcohol. Those who cannot resist temptation tend to satisfy their taste under the cover of darkness. In big cities such as Casablanca and Rabat, young people indulge in alcohol at parties, bars, discotheques, and during private banquets *(diffas)* and celebrations. Moroccan wines are very good and inexpensive. Their special qualities have won them ready markets internationally.

Given the religious prohibitions on alcohol, nonintoxicating beverages and fruit juices *(sharbat)* such as nut, apple, almond, orange, lemon, grape, and pomegranate and mineral waters are popular in Morocco. Coffee is also consumed. Moroccans sometimes add spices to their coffee.

Cuisine and Ceremonies

Moroccans love their food and celebrate their important festivals and ceremonies with eating and drinking. Food is both a necessity for survival and an expression of wealth, class, social nature, and culture. To the Moroccan, food connects with "the finer instincts of life and love as well as the sheer delight in sensual gratification."[10]

In contrast to the preparation of family meals, ceremonial meals are prepared more elaborately. Professional chefs are usually involved in the preparation of dishes intended for guests at special occasions. The host may not participate in the cooking except to provide the required ingredients and instructions. Also, women may not be involved in the preparation of certain meals at such occasions. After the guests are seated at a low table, a ceremonial pouring of perfumed water on three fingers of the guests' right hands is performed, and the host claps his hands before the banquet is served. The three fingers on the right hand are ritually cleaned because Moroccan's eat with their fingers instead of with spoons and forks. For starters at a banquet, a cool fresh salad may comprise a combination of any of the following: eggplant, sliced tomato *(batinjaan)*, green pepper, mixed herbs, and oranges. Oranges are grown in Morocco in large quantities.

In other celebrations, such as weddings, circumcisions, rites of passage, and return from a hajj, women of the house are involved in the preparation of meals. The hostesses dress in long robes tucked in front with the wide sleeves held in place with a twisted cord. The preparation of certain ceremonial meals might take days. This is especially so when the menu involves 20 or 30 courses. The ceremonial dinner may commence with a crisp pigeon pie *(bisteeya)* rolled very thin and sometimes filled with a chicken mixture and prepared in as many layers as desired.[11] The host then serves roasted bits of beef or lamb (kebab) flavored with spices and animal fat. This is accompanied by the traditional spicy stew, *tajine*. The *tajine* is sometimes served with bread *(khubz)*. If not served as an appetizer, then eggplant salad or chopped tomato salad may be served with couscous—which often comes as the main course. After the main course, sliced melon and honey and almond pastries are served as part of a series of desserts, which traditionally ends with several small cups of mint tea.

One special ceremonial meal of Morocco, which is typically Berber in origin, is the traditional whole roasted lamb, or barbecue, known among the Berbers as *mechoui* or *mashwi*. Long before foreign intrusion, most Berber households kept goats, sheep, cattle, and fowl for their dietary needs. Today, goat and sheep remained the major domesticated livestock. Livestock provide a source of meat, butter, milk, and eggs, and they also serve as capital reserve that can easily be converted into cash. In most African indigenous communities, including the countryside *(bled)* of Morocco, meat is rarely part of the everyday family menu; rather, it is reserved for important occasions such as births, initiations, weddings, and burial ceremonies when meat is shared among the members of the community.

The *mechoui* is prepared by rubbing the lamb with garlic, ground cumin, and olive oil and then roasted over a fire until it turns deep brown. This meal is often used to mark the Muslim festival of Aid El Babir, which comes after the month of Ramadan. In another ceremony for the birth of a child, a lamb is killed for a feast on the seventh day after the birth. Male circumcision ceremonies are also marked with a similar celebration. The sumptuous whole-lamb barbecue is expensive and therefore not a common meal for the poor, but it is the main course of a special Moroccan royalty feast known as the *zerda*.

TRADITIONAL DRESS AND FASHION

The Djellaba (or *Zellaba*)

The djellaba is a popular garment originally worn by Moroccans men. Since the mid-twentieth century, the djellaba has become part of women's fashion even beyond Morocco. The djellaba is a type of long outer robe, distinguished by its long sleeves and hood. The most popular color for men is white. A European visitor to Tangier in 1897 described the entire city as having the look of a vast monastery of Dominican monks: "everyone wears a long white linen or woolen cape, furnished with a hood, which in most cases is drawn over the head."[12] This scenario has only changed slightly because the popular white djellaba still remains in vogue. The men's version is made with the sleeves clinging to the arms. In a society where the men often like to shave their heads so they are almost bald, a prominent feature of the dress is a hood, which offers the body protection from the harsh elements of the weather—sand, sun, and moisture. The men also wear a small red cap *(chechiya)* under the hood.

The women's version of the djellaba is a long-sleeved, loose-fitting garment with a hood, large pockets on both sides, and a zipper in front to make it easier to put on and take off. Although there are many regional and class variations of dress for women, the djellaba has become one of the favorite designs for "urban women for attending school or work as well as for other activities."[13]

The Burnoose

The Burnoose is a one-piece cloak worn mainly over loose tunics—that is, a simple pull-on garment that is made with or without sleeves and usually

Zellaba (djellaba) fashion store in the city of Moulay Idris. Courtesy of Valerie Orlando.

knee-length or longer, belted at the waist, and worn by men and women. The burnoose is of Berber origin and traditionally made like a simple robe. It is cut in a half-circle design and has a hood like the djellaba. The hood provides protection from the punishing desert sun and sand. Today, the Berber burnoose has undergone some design changes. Although the latest versions appear remarkably different from the original design, the successful urban executives wear them over business suits in the manner of President Hamid Karzai of Afghanistan.

The Turban

Another important part of men's traditional wear is the turban and the little knit cap with a patterned band around it. A turban is a headdress worn mostly by Muslims in most parts of the eastern Mediterranean, including North Africa and South Asia. Both the turban and the knit cap are worn close to the head. There are brimless so that they do not interfere with bows made during prayers.[14] The turban with the red fez is popular among businesspeople. Rather than the turban, average rural dwellers and ordinary people wear the little round knit caps.

The Caftan

The traditional garment for women is the silk or cotton robe called the caftan, which often comes with gold belts and decorated bands on the edges. It is one of the most popular and perhaps most beautiful of all female attire found in Morocco. Traditionally, it was a long robe that came down to the feet. Today, it is common to find caftans shortened to the ankle and made of any fabric. Some are made with expensive materials and decorated with embroidery. This expensive type is usually reserved for weddings and other special occasions. At weddings, the bride adorns her head with a bright-colored headband. On her feet she wears traditional flat open-heeled slippers *(sbabsushat),* known in French as *babouche* or *babouj,* with tassels and trimmings. The *babouche* is worn by both sexes and it is also popular in Algeria, Tunisia, and some parts of Libya.

The Great Dress *(Kswat el Kebira)*

Among the Jews of Morocco, the women are distinguished by their traditional costume known as the Great Dress *(Kswat el Kebira).* The origin of this attire has been traced back to the Spanish Jews, known as the Sephardim. Following their expulsion in the fifteenth century, those who resettled in Tetuan,

Morocco, made the Great Dress one of their most popular costumes. It is decorated with ornate embroidery in varied colors and comes in several parts. The first is a wrap skirt usually made of velvet with bands of gold embroidery and is called the *jeltita*. In Spain this is known as *giraldetta*. The second part of the Great Dress is an open top with short sleeves known as the *gonbaiz*. The third part is a trimming, like a bracelet, worn inside the *gonbaiz* and called the *punta* or *ktel*. The fourth part of the dress is a shawl *(kmam)* worn over the shoulders. The last part is a belt or girdle *(hzam)* with elaborate and expensive gold embroidery. Originally, the Great Dress was proudly offered as a gift to young maidens from their fathers. It symbolizes parental consent to a daughter's relationship with a prospective suitor. Hence, the Great Dress was initially worn at a prenuptial (henna) ceremony. These days it is fairly common to see young women wear the Great Dress on other special occasions. The dress could now be made of velvets, brocades, and silks.

Adornments

Moroccan women, like women the world over, love to wear jewelry. Heavy earrings, bracelets, anklets, and strings of pearls are some of the common objects of adornment. The women adorn their hands with bracelets of different designs and ornaments. Similarly, those who can afford the costs adorn their legs with anklets made of precious stones. The necklace is both an object of fashion and an object of affluence. Moroccan women love to keep an assortment of expensive trinkets, ranging from the simplest Zagora and Tuareg necklaces to the expensive *maguna* and *coin-coral* jewels.

European Impact

Although Moroccans today mostly dress in their traditional garments and costumes, Western styles of dress are gradually making inroads, especially among the younger generation. It is therefore proper to state that for both the younger and older generations, dressing has become an expression of local as well as global identity or "modernity." For instance, a student may have a wide selection of Western-style shirts, trousers, suits, sportswear, and Italian or Spanish shoes but will maintain his traditional djellaba for going to the Mosque, attending weddings, and for other similar outings. Sometimes, city-dwellers combine Western-style suits and shirts with their traditional robes. It is common to come across men wearing foreign shoes and sneakers in cities like Casablanca and Rabat. European dress began to appear in the second decade of the twentieth century, following French colonial rule in Morocco. Initially, the Moroccan Jews were the first to take to European textiles and fashions, especially trousers, shirts, and hats for men.[15] Today, Western-style dress has significant impact on the way young people dress.

Whereas the women still dress primarily in traditional garments and cover their heads with veils *(pushi)* in respect for religious demands, some, especially the educated women and gender activists with Western contacts, have begun to appear at work, in colleges, and in other public places dressed in jeans and simple shirts or blouses. Also, urban married women are more likely to wear makeup than are single women. This is because most potential bridegrooms are reluctant to marry young women who wear cosmetics and dress like Westerners. A recent study in Casablanca found that these unmarried women are considered untraditional, liberated, wild, and therefore not the "serious" type men look for in wedlock.[16]

Dress and Identity

Moroccans are what they wear. In other words, there is an intricate expression of self in the manner in which Moroccans dress. Traditional dress, like food, art objects, and design, reveals much about a people's cultural heritage— their values, aesthetics, taboos, norms, transmitted culture, adaptations, and shared history. Dress and identity also connect to the economics, politics, and the predominant religion of a society.

For instance, the brimless traditional turban, knit cap, and veil widely worn in Muslim societies reflects not only the religion but also tells something

Young women in the street dressed in Western-style attire. Courtesy of Valerie Orlando.

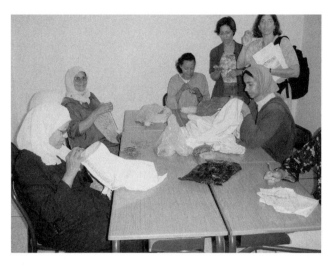

Women wearing traditional long dresses, headscarf, and veils at a literacy program in Ifrane, Morocco. Courtesy of Valerie Orlando.

about the modes of worship in Islam. It allows room for bowing down, without having to adjust the headdress or removing it completely. Similarly, the emphasis on long-sleeved dresses and costumes that fall to the legs have a connection to the Islamic religion. Islam forbids exposure of the human body so as not to tempt the weak of society to indulge in lewd acts; therefore, it is ideal for men and women to wear modest attire. The traditional head scarf and veil worn by women in Muslim societies, including Morocco, encourage the image of women in this part of the world as humble, respectful, and virtuous home managers. Therefore, Moroccan women in seclusion, especially city dwellers, are encouraged to adhere to this tradition. In the countryside and among the Berbers, a scarf, tied around the head, is a more popular kind of covering. In the 1980s, when the number of women who wore the veil declined, the Sufi religious sect immediately launched a revivalist movement. The young people became more prayerful and perceived religion as a "personal anchor when other symbols of identity were under strain." Similarly, many working women came to equate the veil with "personal freedom: they expressed their religious identity by wearing Islamic dress and emphasized their personal identity by working."[17] In the context of decolonization in Morocco (1940s–1956), the scarf represented not only a religious and cultural symbol but also identification with the national liberation struggle because it showed the face. This competing notion of the scarf is now a subject of debate as to whether it is actually a symbol of religion or overarching patriarchal authority and domination.[18] For the more liberated Berber women, the scarf tied around the waist embodies an attempt to define their original non-Arab cultural heritage.

NOTES

1. Catherine Hanger, *World Food: Morocco* (Victoria, Australia: Lonely Planet Publications, 2000), 15–16.

2. Paula Wolfert, *Couscous and Other Good Food from Morocco* (New York: Harper and Row, 1973), 1–3.

3. Roger Joseph and Terri Brint Joseph, *The Rose and the Thorn: Semiotic Structures in Morocco* (Tucson: University of Arizona Press, 1987), 19.

4. Wolfert, *Couscous,* 49–55.

5. Claudia Roden, *A Book of Middle Eastern Food* (New York: Alfred A. Knopf, 1972), 277.

6. The mosses (phylum Bryophyta), seedless vascular plants, come in different varieties. They are found in most geographical zones around the world, including the desert. The leaves have medicinal value.

7. For a detailed treatment on the uses of these herbs, spices, and aromatics, see Wolfert, *Couscous,* 19–32.

8. See Hanger, *World Food,* 15–16.

9. See C. R. Pennell, *Morocco since 1830: A History* (New York: New York University Press, 2000), 260.

10. Hanger, *World Food,* 14.

11. Harold D. Nelson, ed., *Morocco: A Country Study,* 4th ed. (Washington, D.C.: American University Press, 1978), 125.

12. Edmondo De Amicis, *Morocco: Its People and Places,* trans. Maria Hornor Lansdale (Philadelphia: Henry T. Coates, 1897), 5.

13. Susan Ossman, *Picturing Casablanca: Portraits of Power in a Modern City* (Berkeley: University of California Press, 1994), 203. See also Susan Ossman, *Faces of Beauty: Casablanca, Paris, Cairo* (Durham, NC: Duke University Press, 2002).

14. Nelson, *Morocco,* 125–26.

15. Daniel J. Schroeter and Joseph Chetrit, "The Transformation of Eassaoira (Mogador) in the Nineteenth and Twentieth Centuries," in Harvey E. Goldberg, ed., *Sephardi Middle Eastern Jewelries: History and Culture in the Modern Era* (Bloomington: Indiana University Press, 1996), 103, 109.

16. Ossman, *Picturing Casablanca,* 167.

17. Ibid., 364; Mounia Bennani-Chraibi, *Soumis et rebelles: les jeunes au Maroc* (Casablanca: Edition le Fennec, 1994), 89–100; Henry Munson, *Religion and Power in Morocco* (New Haven, CT: Yale University Press, 1993), 162–67.

18. Ossman, *Picturing Casablanca,* 203.

6

Gender Roles, Marriage, and Family

SURVIVING INDIGENOUS BERBER CUSTOMS, Arab and Jewish family practices, and European influences have all combined to form contemporary kinship practices, family organization, marriage traditions, and notions of gender relations in Morocco. With expansion of Western-style education, closer contacts with peoples of other cultures (including Africans, Asians, and Europeans), and continuing changes in socioeconomic structures and individual lifestyles, the Moroccan family has been responding to dynamics that will continue to shape it. Since the 1970s, for instance, most of the newly educated elite, especially those who received their degrees in France, Belgium, Spain, the United States, or other Western countries, have returned home to make marriages and establish what is often referred to as a more "individualistic" family practices. Whereas the emergent class demonstrates a preference for a smaller and easily manageable family size, most Moroccans have continued to follow tradition with a preference for polygamous marriages, large families, and close kinship and family ties.

As a universal institution, the family is both an organic and social unit of acculturation. Members are linked by blood, and new members are incorporated through marriages. For the welfare and continuity of a unit, members often maintain a common residence as well as follow instituted norms for production and reproduction. This communal relationship ensures generational continuity through prescribed codes of sexual relationships. Therefore, similar to what is found in most African and Asian societies, family life is at the center of Moroccan social order, and children are socialized in accordance with family traditions as an integral part of the wider societal values, expectations, taboos, and religion. In most parts of the so-called Third World, where social security rarely exists, the family fills that vacuum, with the more privileged assisting the poorer members with the basic necessities of life. Young people in Morocco live at home and participate in social events arranged by the family until they are old enough to go to school, learn a trade, or pursue a career that may take them away from home.

Traditionally, it is expected that male children will continue to contribute to the welfare of their families; hence, sons tend to remain in their family home after marriage and raise their own families within the extended family structure. In Morocco, however, the sons are free to set up their own households and retain the family's name when the father dies. Although most people still conform to this tradition, the younger generations are gradually opting to live independently with their nuclear families. As it is in most parts of the world, kinship in Morocco is structured along patrilineal lines, the organization of a household based on male blood ties.

LINEAGE

A typical traditional family system retains a link between the present generation and past generations of members who often had lived under the same house or in a compound comprising several households whose members have common blood ties. A household consists of a man, his wife (or wives), and their children, including married sons, their wives, and their children. Other relatives such as unmarried daughters, widows, or divorcées are also accepted as part of the family. In other words, kinship relations, especially among people of Arab and African descent, follow a complex network of relationships linking many families to a common ancestor. Several studies have shown that among the Berbers the word *aith,* meaning "sons of," as encountered with "Aith Waryaghar," "Aith Tuzin," and "Aith Ammarth," implies that members of each of these local communities are connected by blood to one remote ancestor. In contrast with the practice in the United States, for example, where the nuclear family is at the center of family life, the Berbers of the Central Rif Mountains often identified themselves primarily as members of their lineage *(dharfiqth)* comprising several families (*ijujga; singular, jajgu*).[1] Nonetheless, as a survey in 1978 showed, the "extended family appeared to be uncommon in the Middle Atlas and in many other regions as well."[2] Consequently, generalizations are hard to make. Cultural practices are neither rigid nor uniformly the same even among peoples of the same cultural geography. Cultural practices cannot be viewed exclusively from the standpoint of "African" or "Arab" or "Western" contexts but rather in their fluid and dynamic contexts.

In most Berber-Arab patrilineal communities, lineage members, or the extended family, can expect a share in inheritance of a deceased's property. This is in accordance with Islamic practices, which outline heirs in family property to include grandfather/mother, father/mother, and son/daughter. Men, however, enjoy inheritance rights over women, whose share of inheritance often depends on the disposition and generosity of their male relations. Also, lineal relations are favored over collaterals (aunts, uncles, and cousins). In patrilineal family systems, as opposed to matrilineal, all children—boys and girls—belong to the father's kinship group, and married women adopt the family name of their husbands. In many Western societies today, there is a growing tendency for women, especially, among the successful professionals, to retaining their family names after marriage. In Morocco, this is hardly an issue because the married women are still supported financially by their husbands even when some of them may have sources of private income.

MARRIAGE

In all societies, marriage is an important social custom and will continue to be so in the future. Although marriage confers respect and status to single women and young men, its most important function remains for procreation, or reproduction. The institution of marriage provides society with a formal avenue through which new units of households are created, replenishing and reinvigorating aging networks of kinship and lineage systems. In Morocco, married couples will go to any length to ensure that their union is successful, which means having children of their own. Children are the fruits and the main purpose and joy of marriage. In most predominantly agrarian societies, including Morocco, large families are desired to provide sources of labor, to protect against external aggression, and to ensure social security and continued support for members in their old age. As soon as children start arriving in a family, divorce becomes very difficult because both partners become more tolerant of each other to protect the welfare of their children.

Additionally, a marriage is not all about the couple; it brings families together into a new cooperative alliance. Therefore, the family plays a central role in the choice of a marriage partner through participation in the various social and religious rituals connected with the marriage process. The unrelenting intervention of elders in intrafamily schisms further attests to the larger rather than private nature of marriage practices in Morocco.

Traditionally, most parents considered it their responsibility to choose spouses for their children. In a society where the sexes seldom interacted, marriage partners are linked through social contacts or through negotiations involving mothers or even professional matchmakers. Fathers typically are not openly involved in the negotiation and planning stages of weddings, but their consent is usually necessary. Although mothers take the initiative, they first discuss in detail their plans and report to their husbands about progress in the mate selection and bridewealth (a payment from the groom's family to the bride's family) negotiations. The father's consent, as the head of his family, is crucial and cannot be ignored. Although parents negotiate marriages for their children, the groom's consent also comes into consideration before the commencement of wedding details. Traditionally, the bride-to-be plays a more passive role in the decisions, although this tradition is now changing.

Endogamy, or marriage within the larger extended family, is common, "with the preferred marriage partner being the male's first cousin on the father's side (*bint 'amm,* or the father's brother's daughter)."[3] In the central High Atlas region, for instance, marriages often involved parallel cousins or the children of brothers. By securing marriages with their own cousins, it is assumed that the men bring honor, respect, and protection to their families. In other places, such as the Rif, no specific marriage pattern or preference exists, but incestuous relationships are taboo, and intermarriage is often negotiated between

Bride in Marrakech. Courtesy of Valerie Orlando.

families of similar social class. With an increase in Western-style education, contact with foreigners through travels, and the influx of foreign films and television programs, young people in Moroccan are gradually beginning to choose their own partners with minimal parental influence.

Islamic law, in accordance with Quranic stipulation, allows men to marry as many as four wives. Such polygamous relationships, however, are only possible for the privileged because it is financially difficult to maintain a harem. All Moroccans are expected to marry as they come of age. Men normally marry before they are 30 years old, and women usually marry before the age of 18. Women older than 23 may experience great anxiety over getting married.

In contrast with the sacramental idioms of Christian matrimony, marriage in Islam is a civil contract *(aqd)*, and the terms of agreement are more or less determined by the couple's family representatives. The contract stipulates the rules and guidelines that may not be violated. An important part of the contractual agreement is the requirement upon the groom's family to make a monetary payment to the bride's family.

Bridewealth

In most African and Middle Eastern societies, marriage is not considered legal without a negotiated bridewealth or dowry. Whereas the dowry is a personal debt to the bride alone, bridewealth is a payment from the groom's family to the bride's family and often involves a substantial sum of money. In Morocco, the payment of bridewealth is an important part of the wedding process. The rationale for this practice is largely based on the enormous costs parents bear in raising a female child. The groom's family literally owns the bride after marriage, so the idea follows that a bride's parents deserve some form of monetary compensation during her wedding. This practice has been institutionalized as payment of bridewealth or dowry *(dfoua)*. Often the amount involved is so large that it is paid in installments. Some families of the bride are hesitant to ask for the entire dowry until it is needed in the future.[4]

Additionally, the bride's family responds with a kind of dowry with which the bride must enter her husband's home. This money is traditionally used to procure furniture and other household items. Although the woman can hardly initiate a divorce in most Muslim societies, in Morocco, she is permitted to take all household belongings acquired with her father's sponsored dowry, including other items purchased thereafter. As the bridegroom stands to lose everything after divorce, this practice serves as a kind of security for wives against treacherous husbands.

Procedures and Ceremonies

In Morocco, marriage is a ritual, and wedding ceremonies last days. The process, which combines traditional and modern aspects, remains the same throughout Morocco but has minor differences in organization across the regions. In Hadiddou Imilchil of southern Morocco, for instance, the process for the selection of marriage partners may involve either a family-to-family contact or participation in a traditional "wedding fair" where young people come together accompanied by their families to explore the possibility of meeting marriage partners. Once a potential bride has been identified, marriage go-betweens *(khattabat)* are asked to visit the bride's family to estimate her manners, personal attitude, and appearance. They also make a preliminary estimate of the amount of bridewealth her family might demand. Usually, the search for a bride ends with a formal engagement *(khutba* or *khitba)*, which is the first step before marriage celebrations. Couples mark their engagements in diverse ways, depending on family and community traditions.

The groom's family visits their potential in-laws to discuss the marriage plans and settle on a convenient date for the wedding. The preliminary discussions may take several visits, and the process may be terminated at any time. If everything goes according to plan, the settlement of dowry is usually accompanied by the formal signing of the marriage contract. On the arrival of the groom's family, the hosts welcome them with flowers, milk, and dates. The public celebration as determined by religion (whether Islam or Judaism) or cultural expectations then follows.

In Morocco, marriage ceremonies are elaborate and necessary to legalize the wedlock. They assume different forms from family to family and region to region. The sociocultural festivities capture the personal, familial, social, community, and "material/economic life" of the people.[5]

Among the Berbers, marriage ceremonies are part of the people's rituals and value systems. The Berbers draw on natural customs and symbols to give meaning and interpretation to life. Originally, wedding ceremonies lasted for seven days, and the costs of all the celebrations were borne entirely by the bridegroom's family. Because of the enormous financial stress involved, the weeklong marathon wedding festivities have been shortened in most places to three days (commonly called *dhamghra*). A day before the commencement of the public festivities, the bride undertakes a bathing ritual *(nekachat)* that is supposed to purify her body in readiness for the coming rite of passage. Then red and white flags are suspended, respectively, on the roofs of the groom's and bride's family homes. For the groom, the red symbolizes fertility and strength. For the bride, the white represents her virginity and purity.

On the first day, a ceremony called "little henna" *(r-hanni tamzzyant)* is held, starting at the bride's home. Family members, kinsmen, neighbors, friends, and sometimes the entire village are invited for a day of feasting, dancing, and singing. Henna is a reddish brown dye obtained from leaves of the henna plant and it is used especially on hair. In the Berber tradition, the red dye is used on the body. The first-day rituals usually end with the henna ritual, which is primarily intended to protect the couple from evil, attacks from hostile spirits (djinns), or spells cast by enemies. At the bridegroom's home, the red henna dye is prepared and applied to the groom's hands and feet as well as to his wedding attendants *(iwziren)*, whose special role throughout the ceremonies is to protect the groom from dangers. At the bride's home, her younger sister prepares the henna dye, which is also applied to the bride's hands and feet as well as those of her special companions *(dhiwzirin)*.[6]

The second day of celebration is called the "big henna" *(r-hanni amggran)*. Like the first day's events, the big henna also starts at the home of the bride's parents. The celebration continues with eating, singing, and dancing, and both the bride and groom are smeared with generous amounts of the red dye. The bride in particular receives several layers of the dye to adequately prepare her for the impending journey to her new home the next day. This journey is considered to be crucial, and because it is a time when the bride is believed to be most vulnerable to fiendish attacks, all precautions are taken to ward off any unforeseen hazards.

As the third and final day of festivities arrives, the bride departs to her husband's family house with fanfare. This ceremony is also marked with eating and dancing, commencing at the bride's home and ending with the final "night of entry" *(lailat al-dukhla)* held at the husband's family home. The journey begins on the evening of the last celebration after a group of men from the groom's home arrives to fetch the bride. They are welcomed with milk and dates, and the entertainment goes on until late in the night.

In final preparation for the journey, the bride's relatives and friends carefully wrap the bride in a long, white cloth from head to toe in a similar way to how dead people are prepared for burial in most Muslim societies. A long-tasseled handkerchief *(tasebnath)* is hung over a bent twig *(qubbath)* from a grapevine and attached to the bride's head. Her face is carefully covered with her veil, the handkerchief, and the white shroud. The white veil and shroud symbolize the bride's virginity as well as her expected total obedience and submission to her husband. The bridal procession, which is conceived as death, marks the bride's transition from unmarried to married life.[7]

The bridal party departs after the bride's brother has performed his duty to carry his sister to a mule prepared for the journey. The bride's female kin and friends surround the bride and sing, dance, and jubilate. After the bride is seated on the mule, her mother pours barley grains on her lap. The barley seed is associated with fertility, life, and special blessings *(baraka)*. The bride is expected to carry the symbols of this blessing to her new home. As soon as the bride arrives at her husband's home, she spreads the barley seed in front of her new home, signifying that she is bringing prosperity and progress to the two households. Afterward, the bride's brother carries her into a chamber especially reserved for the wedding. Soon after, the groom enters the room to greet his new wife and to remove the handkerchief and the veil.

Following the ceremonies of the last day, the couple is free to consummate their marriage, supposedly for the first time. The focus of the first night of consummation is the expected proof of the bride's virginity, figuratively referred to as the "spill of the blood." Because premarital sex is seriously frowned upon, brides who are found not to be virgins are considered a great shame *(hshuma)* to both families. If the groom is denied the honor to deflower his wife, it is considered enough reason to take such drastic actions as cancellation of the marriage, beating of the bride, or even honor killing. This is only after an arbitration judge has determined the merit of the case, however.[8] The spilling of virginal blood accomplishes the rite of passage and attests to the groom's potency. It confirms the roles of men and women in procreation and initiates the couple into the world of adulthood.[9] For the next seven days after the third and final ceremony, the family of the bride is restricted from seeing her.

Wedding ceremonies in the big cities also draw a large gathering of families, friends, and acquaintances. One slight difference is that the choice of venues may be a popular holiday resort or hotel rather than the urban residential houses. Another difference is that whereas in the countryside there is often an open invitation for members of the village, attendance at most weddings in urban areas is strictly by invitation only. Also, although marriage involves the traditional wedding attire, the contemporary bride and groom might change clothes from the caftan for women and djellaba (or *zellaba*) for men to a white Western-style bridal gown and suit. Some couples may take a honeymoon instead of the traditional seven days of restricted visits that allows the couple some privacy to consummate their wedlock. The recent changes are aspects of the Western impact on wedding ceremonies in North Africa.

Marriage Forms

In accordance with Islamic injunctions, it is legal in Morocco for men to marry as many as four wives, depending on individual lifestyle and capability. In other words, polygyny—the marriage of one man to multiple women—is an accepted social practice. The Quran clearly stipulates, however, that a man must be adequately prepared to treat each of his wives and children with fairness and justice before getting into multiple marriages. This means that the potential polygamist must make sure that he has the economic ability to care for his family and must show his wives equal love. Thus, contrary to popular assumptions, polygamy is strictly for the privileged and not a license for lascivious men to indiscriminately acquire wives. It is the responsibility of a husband in a polygynous household to provide his wives and children with decent accommodations, medical care, and clothing, as well as to meet his wives' sexual needs. Today, many educated women are rebelling against polygynous relationships, and among the new generation, men are beginning to see polygyny as an expensive lifestyle they cannot afford. In this light, one can understand why polygyny may be legal but not widely practiced in Morocco today. Rather, monogamy is gradually becoming the new trend.

Another type of multiple marriage is polyandry, the marriage between a woman and several men. Polyandry in Morocco exists only as a theoretical possibility. In most patriarchal societies, including Morocco, there is no provision for a woman to marry more than one husband without first separating from the first.

DIVORCE

For the Muslim husband, divorce involves a seemingly simple process of repeating the phrase "I divorce thee" three times in the presence of witnesses. This is not as simple as it often appears, however. Provisions may demand that the husband pronounce these words in stages over a considerable period of time during which arbitration is possible and the relationship may be saved. Over this period, paternal fathers, elders, family, and relations may meet to discuss issues and implore the husband and wife to reconsider their decision. It is rare for a woman to seek divorce from her husband because separation is seen in a very negative light, although it is not prohibited. Therefore, the couple must have good reason to entertain a divorce. Often the causes of separation include the inability of the husband to provide proper financial and material support for his wife (or wives) and children; adultery, especially on the part of the wife; and the inability of a wife to bear children, particularly male children. In any of these circumstances, a man may decide to acquire another wife or seek a divorce. When every effort to save a relationship fails to result in reconciliation, a local judge (qaid) may grant a divorce. If the judge finds the husband guilty of wrongdoing or maltreatment of his wife, he must pay a settlement that is part of the bridewealth and forfeit the furnishings of the house brought by his wife. Additionally, the treacherous husband may be required to pay his former spouse a maintenance allowance for three months *(sqaq)*. If the woman is found guilty, especially in the case of adultery, she forfeits the *sqaq* and household furnishings.

After the separation, the law usually permits children of the couple to remain with their father. Some flexibility is allowed, however, to help reduce the psychological and physiological impact on minors. For instance, after divorce, children older than age two may either live with their father or with their mother until their father remarries. Those younger than two, especially girls, may remain with their mother, but they must return to their father when they come of age or when their mother remarries.[10]

FAMILY AND GENDER ROLES

Male-female relationships in most Muslim societies are patterned in a way that may be perceived as constituting separate subsocieties. In Morocco, however, this form of social organization has been gradually changing since the 1990s. For instance, a 1993 study on the Zawiya of central Morocco revealed that coeducational public institutions, popular music, television, and travel to urban centers are gradually altering sexual attitudes and practices in these communities as the sexes come into closer contact.[11] The importance of males in society is expressed primarily in the expectation of wives to bear sons. Failure on the part of wives to meet this expectation sometimes constitutes enough reason for the husband to either seek a divorce or embark on a polygamous relationship.

The attitude and role of women in society are largely informed by the people's worldview, their customs, including prevalent economic, demographic, and political culture.[12] In general, men enjoy a higher social status and appear to dominate the women in certain aspects of life. A stereotypical notion of a woman's role is to care for her children and the household. It is her responsibility to shop, cook, feed, and educate the children while the man is away at work. Moroccan women maintain a clean house, and during their leisure time they may visit family members, friends, or attend prayers at the neighborhood shrines or mosques. Even in the countryside, where Berber women share the agricultural duties with their husbands and do not wear restrictive veils, they are still obligated to conform to their primary responsibilities of childcare and food preparation. Also, Muslim women rarely accompany their husbands to social events outside the household, especially because they have so many responsibilities in the house to occupy their day. Whereas men live a much more unstructured life, women are expected, but not forced, to adhere to certain codes of behavior, especially before marriage. For instance, it is considered crude for young women to marry outside their race or faith, to travel abroad without obtaining parental consent, or to be unaccompanied late at night. In Morocco, it is forbidden for the predominantly Berber-Arab women to be married to either French, Spanish, or Jewish men, but their men are free to marry outsiders. Unlike men, women are scolded for smoking in public. When a wife errs, it is also part of the culture for a man to beat her—an act considered abuse in Western societies.

The notion of male domination is neither as simplistically assumed by outsiders nor uniformly practiced. As a study notes, "a closer examination of the structure and operation of the household reveals the presence of a considerable measure of 'unassigned power' which women compete for and utilize to further their own needs and wishes."[13] For instance, a woman's age and status within the household play an important role in her influence and decision making in society. Older women are highly respected and often enjoy the support of their children. They are honored and revered as wise, responsible, and trustworthy. Also, whereas Berber women may have more freedom in the countryside, some educated urban women enjoy relative respect and freedom than do their less educated cohorts. Similarly, uneducated men perform more traditional forms of labor than their educated counterparts. A 1997 study by the International Food and Agricultural Development (IFAD) in the Taforalt-Taourist region of Oujda Province in eastern Morocco has shown that whereas women generally aspire to the lifestyle of a "rich woman," which implies not having to perform menial tasks such as weaving, water collection, and animal husbandry, men and women from the poorer households compromise on these issues in the interest of their families.[14]

In the past, the public spheres of government, law, warfare, and trade used to be the exclusive domains of men. Today, government and commerce involve the active participation of women who serve as political delegates, ambassadors, airline pilots, company directors, and royal advisors. Some women have established themselves as eminent scholars, world athletes, writers, publishers, journalists, and activists. Also, through intrigue and exercise of feminine power, women sometimes get their way. Some wives may resort to witchcraft (*shor* or *s'hur*) or intrigue in an attempt to influence their husbands to love them and not resort to polygamy.

Patriarchal authority still dominates the social order in Morocco, but, overall, gender discrimination has lessened. Women are now free to pursue university education, and their career prospects have continued to expand.

SOCIALIZATION

One of the primary roles of Moroccan families involves the socialization of the younger members into certain dominant sociocultural values and practices. Most families in Morocco do not compromise the traditional expectations shaped by the broad social forces of religion, language, gender, socioeconomic status, birth order, family, and community and such individual factors as tolerance, anxiety, imagination, and identification. Children are raised in the family to respect these traditions as sacred. Practices such as taking care of the elderly tend to guarantee continuities in terms of welfare and provide an avenue for a better and more secure future for all. Therefore, tradition inculcates in the younger members of the society the value that it is not only moral to respect and take care of the weak and elderly but it makes clear to the young that by respecting this practice, a future in which such a patronage will be extended to them is guaranteed.

Families also stress the overarching importance of membership in a kinship group and identification of members with their immediate community. The aim is to prevent people from seeing themselves as individuals accountable only to themselves. The extended family offers members succor and protection in times of bereavement, hardship, and other trials of life. The younger members of the kinship group are therefore expected to remain close to the group and grow to a position where they will replace the departed elders and act as the patriarchs or guardians of the group.

This position is preceded by different stages of development and maturity. Therefore, adulthood can be marked by initiation ceremonies—namely birth, baptism or naming ceremony, circumcision, marriage, parenthood, and so on. For women, the transition to adulthood lies with marriage, which requires adequate preparation. As young children, girls are not discriminated against, but with the onset of puberty, girls are separated from the boys—a precautionary step to safeguard the young women's virginity and to ready them for their future roles as mothers. As early as possible, mothers begin to educate their daughters in the art of home management. In most African societies, including Morocco, marriage is held as the crowning moment of a woman's life. Therefore, adequate preparation is the norm rather than the law. Years before their suitors arrive, girls begin to participate in the wedding ceremonies of their older sisters, cousins, and friends. They internalize the procedures as they participate in the rituals of singing, dancing, and feasting that usually mark the beginning of married life. Early in their childhood, girls are also introduced to veiling as a proper way of dressing for the woman. Such traditional modes of dress add a measure of respect both to the woman and to her family. More importantly, Muslim girls are trained to perceive sex outside marriage as dangerous to the social order. Although marriage is conceived as the essential part of adult life, the seclusion of women serves to keep indiscriminate sexuality under control. The family rather than any formal institution educates children in this social culture.

As adults, the children join different male or female groups, occupational guilds, religious orders, and different professional careers in accordance with individual interests. Some of these professions may require special skills for memberships and therefore are not open to all. Again, the family is in the best position to advise its members on the best course of action toward attaining success in career goals. Therefore, occupational groups are important to children and adults alike. High-status families expect their members to maintain the family honor through lofty aspirations and achievements. It is not uncommon for poorer families to equally expect their members to overachieve. The idea behind all the pressure for conformity or overachievement is to preserve family honor.

Social Change

From the beginning of European colonialism in 1912 to the end of colonial rule in 1956 and after, Morocco has seen much social change. With expansions in Western-style education, a new global cash economy, sophisticated bureaucracy, the emergence of new political demands, and increased opportunities for social mobilization, many people have started to reject the demands of communal life in favor of notions of individuality, and old family ties continue to break down. Also, as the government pushes its modernization agenda in an attempt to lower levels of illiteracy, unemployment, and poverty, the educated and younger generations increasingly opt to set up their own independent households upon marriage, free from parental and kinship controls. Other strong inducements of social change include television, radio and cassettes, books, films, travel, and, recently, the Internet.

The Western-educated elite have been profoundly influenced by Western ideas so that many of them now view polygamy as an aberration. The urban environment, Western-style education, and modern economies tend to make monogamy the most common arrangement among the elite, especially as they desire, like their counterparts in other societies, to maintain a higher standard of living. For this group, the age has passed when the size of one's family served as a standard for measuring success in society. These days, what matters most is one's professional career. Moreover, other physical manifestations of success, including the type of car (or cars) one drives, manner of dressing, or ownership of a successful business, palatial residential houses, and even one's connections to Europe or other Western countries, have become important to some of the younger generation.

Another aspect of social change in Morocco can be observed in how wedding celebrations have transformed in recent times. Traditionally, weddings in Muslim societies and African societies in general are marked with lavish banquets and expensive dresses and adornments. As the economy experiences downturns, couples are making do with simple ceremonies. Also, it is no longer out of the ordinary for young people to live together after their formal engagement. In the past, a formal engagement ceremony came a year before the actual wedding. These days, especially in the urban centers, an engagement may assume the place of the wedding itself, similar to what is practiced in the United States and Europe, thereby demonstrating that the bride's premarital virtue is not an issue. Additionally, the expectation of female virginity is gradually changing as a result of increasing stress and anxiety over conformity. A recent study in the Zawiya area shows that there have been cases where couples who have been sexually active before their weddings either brought their own blood, cut themselves, or even sneaked in animal blood into the bedroom to display as a sign of virginity.[15]

Another recent study noted, within households, professional working mothers are beginning to spend more time away from home. According to a Moroccan woman writer, a large number of women, especially those in the cities, now have freer access to higher education that was denied them in the past. As a consequence, these women tend to pursue different professional careers after their training.[16] Such professions as law and journalism allow the women little time to raise large numbers of children. Although most Moroccan men, especially the less educated in the Western sense, still prefer to have a traditional housewife, marrying an educated wife with a growing career has become a source of prestige, especially among the Westernized elite.

The most remarkable changes are those concerning the status of women in society. With the increasing voices of protest coming from Western-educated women who are also social activists and writers, women are beginning to participate more in activities outside the home. For instance, although most women still wear veils, others tend to dress more freely, including adoption of Western-style clothing. The majority who still adhere to the veil do so more out of tradition than by compulsion. Although Moroccan women appear to enjoy more freedom than do women in many other Muslim societies, there is still room for improvement in the quest to raise women's status and protect their rights.

Notes

1. Roger Joseph and Terri Brint Joseph, *The Rose and the Thorn: Semiotic Structures in Morocco* (Tucson: University of Arizona Press, 1987), 28; Ernest Gellner, *Saints of the Atlas* (London: Weidenfeld and Nicholson, 1969), 66; David M. Hart, "The Tribe in Modern Morocco: Two Case studies," in Ernest Gellner and Charles Micaud, eds., *Arabs and Berbers: From Tribe to Nation in North Africa* (London: Duckworth, 1972), 28.

2. Harold D. Nelson, ed., *Morocco: A Country Study* (Washington, D.C.: American University Press, 1978), 118–119.

3. Carolyn Fluehr-Lobban, *Islamic Societies in Practice,* 2nd ed. (Gainesville, University of Florida Press, 2004), 98.

4. For more details, see Nelson, *Morocco,* 119.

5. Robert Elbaz, "Toward a Comprehensive Socio-Cultural Theory of the Jewish Life-World in Morocco: The Jewish Traditional Marriage in Morocco," *Extenza: International Journal of Francophone Studies* 7, no. 1 (June 2004): 95–101.

6. Joseph and Joseph, *Rose and the Thorn,* 59–61.

7. Ibid., 60–61.

8. M. E. Combs-Schilling, *Sacred Performances: Islam, Sexuality, and Sacrifice* (New York: Columbia University Press, 1989), 216.

9. See Combs-Schilling, *Sacred Performances,* 206–207.

10. Vanessa Maher, *Women and Property in Morocco* (Cambridge: Cambridge University Press, 1974), 193–202.

11. See Douglas A. Davis and Susan Schaefer Davis, "Sexual Values in a Moroccan Town," in W. J. Lonner and R. S. Malpass, eds., *Psychology and Culture* (Needham Heights, MA: Allyn and Bacon, 1993), 225–230.

12. Rachel Simon, "Between the Family and the Outside World: Jewish Girls in the Modern Middle East and North Africa," *Jewish Social Studies* 7, no. 1 (2000): 81–108.

13. Amal Rassam, "Women and Domestic Power in Morocco," *International Journal of Middle Eastern Studies* 12 (1980): 171.

14. International Food and Agricultural Development, *Survival, Change and Decision-Making in Rural Households: Three Village Case Studies from Eastern Morocco* (Rome: IFAD, 1997), 1–2.

15. Davis and Davis, "Sexual Values," 226–229.

16. Fatima Agnaou, *Gender, Literacy, and Empowerment in Morocco* (New York: Routledge, 2004).

7

Social Customs and Lifestyle

AMID A PLURALITY OF social customs and practices in Morocco are festivities that commemorate family events such as the birth of a child, circumcision, marriage, death, and the return of a member from a pilgrimage to Mecca (hajj). Major religious festivals and holidays include events marking the birth of Muhammad, the holy Prophet of God (or Eid el Mouloud), the end of Ramadan (Eid el-Seghir or Eid el Fitr), and Abraham's sacrifice of a sheep to God instead of his son (Eid el Kebir). Others are occasions that renew community bonds, sports and musical competitions, and commemorations of national unity such as Independence Day and Green March Day. Cultural lifestyles mirror the resilience of indigenous occupational practices and culture as well as emergent Western types of lifestyles rooted in the modern economy.

Traditionally, Moroccans are gregarious, and friendships are best attested to in the existence of a diverse and pervading sense of religious and familial brotherhood. Dramatic salutations such as hugs, kisses, and prolonged handshakes are manners through which people express their sense of hospitality and feelings. A visitor to the traditional open markets in Morocco may find the atmosphere charged with varied forms of activities and excitement—intellectual, sporting, and religious discussions, catcalls, commercial haggling, gossip and laughter, music of singers and dancers, intersections of prayers, chanting by magicians, acrobats, storytellers, snake charmers, circus monkeys, and frequent shouts of ceremonial greetings or obeisance (*ahlan wa sahlan* or *assalaam*). These aspects of customs and lifestyles reflect the diversity of the social setting and extensive knowledge of the people about their society and the world around them. It is common to find Moroccans who consistently follow events around the world via the various modern channels of communication, including the radio, newspaper, television, cable networks, and Internet media. Generally, school children in Africa, including Morocco, are taught more about the wider world than are their counterparts in the United States.

Social and group *(jama'a)* interaction is important whether as part of a religious, political, or cultural community. Generally, individualism gives way to family and community interests. Social gatherings are celebrated in a variety of ways within at least the minimum standards acceptable in Islam. Whatever their background, Muslims, Jews, Christians, Arabs, Berbers, Africans, Europeans, and other groups in the country celebrate events with family, friends, and acquaintances. On such occasions, the hosts demonstrate their generosity with the provision of food, beverages, and music.

SOCIAL RELATIONS

Interpersonal relations follow a code of behavior that places emphasis on respect or dignity *(karama)*, generosity *(karim)*, honor *(sharaf)*, sharing, and hospitality. Religious customs are of the utmost importance and influence day-to-day life. Ideally, the expectations of good morals and ethical standards of honesty are considered integral parts of interpersonal relationships. Due in part to the Muslim practice of feeling great responsibility for guests, the scarce resources of the desert environment, as well as the extraordinary respect of indigenous Africans for strangers, hospitality is so high in all regions of Morocco that it has become a central part of society. It is common for the country folk to invite strangers and acquaintances to their homes for lunch or dinner. At such occasions, the visitor is offered choice items such as meat and other delicacies that are not part of the family's everyday menu. If the stranger is a man, he should not expect the women of the house to join the males at the table, and the visitor is expected not to ask why. The visitor should not use the left hand to eat because that is considered offensive in the culture. In both Islamic and African cultures, the left hand is reserved for handling things considered unclean. Usually, meals are served at home from a communal plate. It is polite for visitors to take only what is immediately in front of them and to accept all that is offered.

CEREMONIES

Ceremonies in Morocco involve formalized series of acts set by ritual, protocol, or convention. Some of the everyday ceremonies are associated with rites of passage; others are connected with the people's belief systems.

Through ceremonies, individual participants demonstrate their respect for conventional acts of politeness or social etiquette. As observers in the prescribed ceremonial procedures, individuals are able to reaffirm their commitment to others and to their customs. Ceremonies are full of action, songs, dancing, prayers, and merriment.

In Morocco, the arrival of a child is celebrated with a lamb feast on the seventh day following the birth. It is usually an occasion for parents, grandparents, uncles, aunts, cousins, and other family and friends to come together and rejoice in the arrival of their newest member. Elaborate prayers are offered, and the lamb meal is part of the ritual to welcome the newborn to the society. Often the child's name is selected to reflect either his or her family history and/or religious identity. For most parents, names such as Mohammed (or Muhammad), Essbai, Musa (Moses), Ali (Noble), Suleyman (Solomon), and Fatima (the Prophet Muhammad's daughter) are preferred. Long names, such as Abu Abdallah Muhammad Ibn Muhammad Ibn Abdallah Ibn Idris al Qurtubi al-Hasani (c. 1100–1165), the much-revered botanist and geographer, tell a deeper history of the bearer's family genealogies, religious identity, and his or her place of birth. In a patrilineal society, the child takes the first name of the father (e.g., Musa Ibn Essbai means Musa, the son of Essbai).

In accordance with Abrahamic practices, the male infant is circumcised soon after birth. Although circumcision is not specifically mentioned in the Quran, most Islamic societies, like their African and Jewish counterparts, practice the removal of the foreskin of the penis at infancy. Although not widely practiced in Morocco, female circumcision takes the form clitoridectomy, or excision of the clitoris, which can be done in infancy or at puberty. For the male, the circumcision ritual introduces the newborn into the culture and religion of his local community. For the female, it marks an important preparation for the adult role she will play as a married woman. As part of the initiation ceremony, a feast is held for the child, who is dressed in traditional clothes, and guests shower the baby with gifts and money. Although most children are circumcised at infancy, some parents may not observe this rite of passage until their children are four years or older. In this case, the observance coincides with the age when the boy is old enough to spend a little more time with his father and other adult males, and he may also accompany the family elders to the mosque.[1] Similarly, a girl who undergoes a clitoridectomy at puberty starts to spend more time in the company of her mother and other adult female members of the kinship group in preparation for her future married life.

As in other Muslim societies, traditional Quranic education is a highly valued part of the developmental stages of life in Morocco. Until recently, the focus of education has been on the training of the learner to master recitation of the

Quran. The ability of the learner to complete the memorization of the Quran is considered a fundamental part of his or her upbringing and development. Such an occasion is marked with a weeklong celebration. The graduating students, with their families, teachers, and friends, parade through their immediate neighborhood reciting prayers and hymns. As the procession passes, neighbors salute the students with gifts. Usually, the proud parents slaughter a sheep and prepare dishes for their family and friends. Today, Quranic education is still an important part of Moroccan life, but Western-style education has taken a position of preeminence because it best equips the individual with the skills to succeed in the modern economy. Therefore, some Moroccans now celebrate the graduation of their sons and daughters from colleges and universities with prayers of thanksgiving, banquets, music, and dances.

Ceremonies that mark the transition to adulthood, such as a wedding, are observed as a community event. Marriage is one of the most important ceremonies in Morocco. It is the crowning of life expectations for the couple as well as their families and kin. Therefore, lavish weddings are still the norm rather than the exception. Because of individual differences in lifestyle, class, level of Western-influence, educational attainment, and family background, however, wedding celebrations vary. More of the younger generation are beginning to shy away from the traditional lavish marriage banquets, opting for a more moderate celebration.

Funeral ceremonies *(salatul janazah)* mark the end of the life cycle of initiations or rites of passage. In the Islamic world, the dead *(Al-Dafin)* are given a simple and quick burial, often before sundown after they are pronounced clinically dead. As a tradition, it is compulsory that a divine service, which is conducted outside the mosque, be held in honor of the dead for the eternal repose of his or her soul and those of all dead Muslims. The body is purified with ceremonial washing by an individual of the same sex, then it is wrapped in a shroud. An exception to this elaborate process of preparation is when the dead is considered a martyr. Martyrs are usually buried unwashed, and their bodies are not customarily wrapped in a white shroud. They are buried in the state in which they died as a testimony to their cause, because they expect a reward for their bravery and sacrifice.

Burial in Morocco is both a family and a community affair. As the burial procession passes, prayers are recited, and sympathizers are expected to join the mourners in reciting the prayers and to help carry the corpse (at least to a certain distance) in the journey to its final resting place. Only the deceased's male relatives are expected to put the body in the grave, and the corpse is laid with its face positioned toward Mecca. A coffin may be used to carry the dead, but they body in not buried in it. The faithful continue to remember the deceased in prayers for several days, asking God (Allah) to be merciful upon his soul. Because Islam teaches of life after death, the mourning of the dead is often brief. As part of the emergent folk Islam in Morocco, ceremonies for the dead are continued as saintly veneration of the Marabouts. In this context, life after death takes a different dimension with the notion of special blessings or rare divine favors *(baraka)* that are said to emanate from saints and noble men to whom certain local communities and neighborhoods attach themselves. *Baraka* is part of everyday life, a concrete manifestation of God's will, and it is invoked to explain how some things occur.[2] For the Western-educated elite, however, this form of loyalty to local saints is becoming outdated.

Other key celebrations that fall within the category of family events is the commemoration of the return of a member from the annual religious pilgrimage to Mecca, called the hajj. The journey to Mecca, in observance of one of the five pillars of the Islamic faith, often is an arduous task. Moroccans who can afford the costs of the journey join millions of pilgrims from more than 70 Muslim countries. The journey from Morocco across the Mediterranean to Saudi Arabia via Cairo or Baghdad or even right through the Red Sea involve great distances and enormous dangers posed by storms, thieves, and possible political unrest in the countries along the way. In the past, pirates and robbers waylaid convoys of pilgrims. It is not unusual for people who traveled by camel or by boat to die. Today, the option of flying has drastically reduced the dangers of road and sea transportation, but the possibility of death by suffocation, trampling, or dehydration during the annual event in Mecca still confronts the pilgrims. Given these risks, the successful return of a member from the arduous but obligatory trip is an occasion for celebration and thanksgiving with family members, neighbors, and friends. Usually, the hosts provide food, drinks, and music, and prayers of thanksgiving are profusely offered on behalf of the returned pilgrim. After his return, the male pilgrims take thee title *al-haji*, and the female assume the title *al-haja*.

Cultural and National Festivals

Moroccans have diverse festivals and holidays embedded in religious values, national events, folklore, and popular culture. Usually, with the approval of the king, each of the big religious and national celebrations is observed with two days of holiday. The dates for most of these annual events are not fixed as they are in the Western calendar introduced by Pope Gregory XIII in 1582. This is because the lunar calendar or a cycle of agricultural harvests determines the dates. In Islam, religious holidays strictly follow the lunar calendar in which each month begins with the sighting of the new moon. Therefore, the various holidays do not fall on the same day each year. Despite the fact that religious festivals are determined by the lunar calendar, civil life in Morocco is organized in accordance with the contemporary calendar, in which the weekend consists of Saturday and Sunday. Also, Moroccans do not consider Friday as a work-free day as the people do in most Islamic states, though the government and private businesses extend their lunch breaks to allow worshippers enough time to observe their Friday prayers. Moroccans celebrate their festivals with prayers and parades of gorgeous traditional dress, song, dance, good food, and drink. Unlike in most Islamic states, the prohibition of alcohol is not strictly enforced, and young people and others take their fill during some private and public parties.

Among the most widely celebrated of the religious festivals in Morocco are Eid el Kebir (or Kabir or Eid el Adbha), Ramadan, Eid el Mouloud, Eid el Muharram, and the various festivals or *mousseums,* which include the popular annual horse-riding festival. These festivities are observed in accordance with time-honored, prescribed rituals in the form of prayers, sumptuous feasts, music, dancing, parades, and fireworks. Eid el Kebir is one of the oldest and most significant religious festivals of the Islamic world, which comes around in late January or February or early March every year. It commemorates the story of Abraham's steadfast readiness to sacrifice his only son, Isaac (or Ishmael), as commanded by God. It is such an important festival that shops, restaurants, and other businesses close in honor of the occasion. Muslims around the world perceive Eid el Kebir as a period to demonstrate unflinching obedience and surrender to God, in keeping with Abraham's example, through acts of gift giving, maintaining promises, and making extra sacrifices. The festival falls during the same period that Muslims observe the traditional pilgrimage to Mecca (hajj). On Eid el Kebir, some families who can afford it usually slaughter a sheep or ram for the celebration. Weeks before the celebration, the animals are conspicuously tethered in every neighborhood. The head of the family leads in the sacrifice by turning the head of the animal toward Mecca before cutting its throat. This is in imitation of Abraham's injunction from God to substitute a sheep for the sacrifice of his son. The meat is meticulously prepared, and all parts of the animal are used in special dishes and barbecue. In accordance with the traditions of the Prophet, all the meat should be divided into three parts to share. A third is distributed to other families and friends as a gift. Another third is specifically reserved for the poor, and the family observing the feast keeps the remainder.

The Eid el fitr (also called Eid el-Seghir or Eid-el-fetr) feast marks the end of Ramadan, which is similar to the Lenten period in Christianity.[3] Because the date is determined according to the lunar calendar, the feast falls on a different day each year. In 2005, the Eid el Fitr will be celebrated on either

November 1 or 4 (1st Shawwal). This date may change depending on when the moon is sighted. However, experts have established November 4 as the most likely day. This festival is typically observed within individual Muslim families. During the month of Ramadan, the ninth month of the Islamic calendar, the Muslims are enjoined to fast *(saum)* and to perform prayers. Ramadan marks the period during which the Quran was revealed to the Prophet Muhammad. By law, Moroccans are prohibited from any acts that imply open contempt of fasting, and it is usual to have a number of young people jailed for this infraction each year. During the month of Ramadan, the people are forbidden to eat, drink, smoke, chew gum, and have sex between sunrise and sunset. They are also prohibited from fighting, lying, and speaking ill of others and should avoid unnecessary arguments. At the end of this period of religious reflection and spiritual renewal, the people celebrate their success-ful fulfillment of the difficult religious obligation with exchanges of felicita-tions such as "Have a happy and blessed Eid-el-fitr" (or *Eid-al-fitr Mubarak*). The participants appear in new clothes, attend fairs, pay visits to friends and associates, enjoy sumptuous feasts, and share special prayers together. The Eid el fitr prayer, which begins shortly after sunrise, is held in large mosques or in an open field to allow for the participation of thousands of worshippers. At the end of the prayers, the people go home to break their fast, and after-ward the celebrations begin. Most families who can afford it are expected to honor the Islamic obligation of giving material or monetary gifts to the poor.

Eid el Muharram (or Moharem) comes exactly three months after the end of Ramadan. Muharram marks the beginning of the Muslim New Year. It is equiva-lent to the New Year's celebration in the Gregorian, or Western, calendar. Again, the date for the celebration is not fixed because of the variations in the lunar calendar, but it usually comes between February and March. For the majority Moroccan Muslims, the Sunni—those who adhere strictly to the teachings and traditions of the holy Prophet of Allah—the beginning of the Islamic calen-dar is observed as a one-day event. The 10th day of the month of Muharram, known as Ashura (or *rawda-khan*) is remembered as the day God saved the Prophet Moses (Musa) from Pharaoh (Fir awn). For the Shiites—those who see Caliph Ali, the Prophet Muhammad's son-in-law, as the rightful inheri-tor of the Caliphate of Islam–Muharram is commemorated with a 10-day period of mourning for the death of Hussein (or Husayn), Ali's son, who was killed at the battle of Karbala in modern Iraq in 680 c.e. According to the Shiites, the killing of Hussein quashed the expectation that Ali's descendents would eventually lead the Muslim world. The Shiites observe Muharram with passionate expressions of grief in the form of plays, songs, beating of chests, and solemn processions that often involve individuals inflicting pain and inju-ries on themselves. Additionally, some Shiites make a pilgrimage to Karbala,

Iraq, where Hussein was killed. The 10th and last day of Muharram marks the climax of the celebrations when the Shiites remember the actual date of Hussein's death.

The annual Eid el Mouloud is usually held anywhere between May and June (depending on the lunar calendar) and commemorates the birth of the Prophet Muhammad. The festival is equivalent to Christmas in Christianity. In Morocco, the event is observed with a big show in the national capital Rabat-Sale (also known as Dar as Salaam) involving a candle-lit parade. Moroccans perceive Eid el Mouloud as a period of excitement and joy. It is celebrated with special prayers and visits to family, friends, and associates. During this period, the people demonstrate their hospitality by providing food and entertainment for their guests.

From September to the end of October, a series of festivals, or *mousseums* (or *ammougars*), are observed across Morocco. The diverse *mousseums* serve as one of the most popular tourist attractions in Morocco today. One of them, a typical Sufi festivity, is a neighborhood-based event in honor of the numerous local Marabouts, or folk saints, whose tombs are found across the country. The celebrations are often held near the tombs of the individual saints. Some small *mousseums,* however, are occasions to observe special market days or harvest periods such as the popular Goulimine market, which is held at the tip of the Sahara to the south. The Goulimine market is famous for its Saturday Tuareg camel market. The Tuaregs are better known as "Blue Men" because of their blue robes and bodies painted with indigo. The weekly market provides the predominantly sedentary local population with an occasion for cultural expression as well as to buy and sell. It is also home to tricksters and the celebrated Guedra dancers, whose mesmerizing rhythms have often been featured in international films.

Others festivities attract interest from far and near. A popular local event is the Berber Bridal Imilchil festival held annually around the third week in September near the burial site of Sidi Mohammed Maghani (also called M'aa-Al Ainine). The festival commemorates the life of the much-admired patron saint of the Ait Haddidou of the Atlas Mountains. The occasion draws various ethnic groups. The people come together to dance, sing, eat, and offer prayers to their patron saint, hoping that the special *baraka* that is believed to coalesce around his tomb will bring them special favors, including success, healing, fertility, and good health. During the festival, the local Berber women adorn themselves in colorful traditional outfits and silver jewelry. The occasion, which was formally an exclusive family affair, presents unmarried women with a forum to find a possible spouse. The common belief is that all the marriages contracted at this festival are blessed by the patron saint, which means that they are happy and successful marriages.

Some cultural celebrations have less intense religious significance. For instance, between June and July falls the annual weeklong national Folklore Festival (or Festival of Arts) held at the ruins of the sixteenth-century Badi palace of the Sa'adi dynasty (1550–1668).[4] The arts festival has become one of the growing tourist attractions in Morocco, and it is graced by dancers, storytellers *(hakawati)*, musicians, artists, acrobats, dancers, painters, craftsmen, vendors, snake charmers, and fire-eaters, who all provide entertaining performances. Among other special attractions of the festival is a choreographed horse-riding spectacle or fantasia. This rich display of horsemanship originally was held in the town of Tissa, which lies about 46 kilometers north of Fès, but since 1976, it has been held annually in Meknès, also a neighboring town, lying to the south of Fès. The festivity, which is held in September, commences with a parade involving local women from the Zayaan region riding on horseback, followed by their men. Soon after the procession comes the so-called Festival of Gunpowder (Eid el Broud), which, as the name suggests, involves explosions and gunfire. Meanwhile, the riders are organized in formations according to their individual rank, and no sooner has one wave of riders left than the next follows, thus displaying surging waves of galloping hooves. The rapid movement of horses is accompanied by the cries of riders and snapping orders from their leader until the whole show explodes in another blaze of gunfire from their homemade rifles, known as *moukhahla.* At the end of the riders' display, prizes are given for the best performers, followed by music and dancing in a large hall.

Early October is a period of harvest, and the festival of the oblong-shaped dates (or festival of the desert fruit) is held in Erfoud, which lies to the east of Meknès. Here, approximately one million date palms of different varieties are harvested annually. The date is a popular delicacy in Morocco, and the local people who grow them rely heavily on the income they generate. It affords the people an occasion to celebrate their agricultural successes with family and friends. During the event, food is served and there are cultural displays of music and dance.

In addition to religious and cultural festivals, Morocco has about four key secular holidays. They remind the people as a nation about their recent political history, including their freedom from European colonial rule and the controversial relationship with neighboring Western Sahara. Although Morocco regained independence on March 2, 1956, when the treaty of Fès ended, the sovereign nation was proclaimed with King Mohammed V emerging as the head of state, on March 3, 1956, in commemoration of the date Mohammed V changed his sultanate to a monarchy. Moroccans, however, usually observe their Independence Day on November 18. This day is set aside as a national holiday, in respect for the sacrifices made by their national heroes and heroines toward freedom from French colonial rule. The second secular national holiday, known as Throne Day, marks the anniversary of King Hassan II's accession to power in 1961. The celebration is observed on March 3. The third national day is Green March Day, which commemorates November 6, 1975, when about 524,000 men and women voluntarily answered the call of their king to march into Western Sahara to claim it for Morocco at the end of Spanish colonial rule in the region. Today, that historic march is perceived as a significant demonstration of Moroccan nationalism. Reunification Day (although historically linked with Green March Day) is the fourth national holiday and commemorates Morocco's declaration of unity with Western Sahara on August 14, 1979.

Old and new forms of cultural and national festivals are emerging to accommodate the dynamics of social change. In recent times, for instance, the ancient city of Fès has become the host of the Festival of World Sacred Music (Festival des musiques sacrées du monde). The annual festival allows the people the opportunity to listen to diverse musical traditions from around the world, including the sacred tunes from the Middle East and the West. This one-week event offers exhibitions, lectures, and intellectual and artistic performances, from Sufi dervishes of Turkey, Arab Andalusian music, Berber trance music, Celtic sacred beats, Christian gospel music, Hindustani chants, and the Morocco Philharmonic.

AMUSEMENT AND SPORTS

Moroccans enjoy their sports and leisure activities. Some of their popular games and pastime activities include skiing, swimming, basketball, hunting, fishing, trekking, golf, and track and field. The most popular sport in Morocco, however, like in most African and European countries is football (soccer). The Moroccan national team, popularly called the Atlas Lions (Les Lions de l'Atlas), remains one of the most respected national teams from Africa, with a record of achievements. In the 1998 World Cup, for example, the Atlas Lions were the first African team to almost make it to the quarter-finals. Morocco has produced world-class footballers who were also voted as African footballers of the following years: Mohammed Timouini (1985), Mustapha Hadji (1998), and Ahmed Faras (1975). The government's strong support of soccer is best attested to by its several but unsuccessful attempts to host the World Cup competition at a state-of-the-art stadium named after the late King Mohammed V, which was constructed in Casablanca in the mid-1990s.

Morocco has produced world-class athletes. Among them is Hicham el Guerrouj, a world-class middle-distance runner who won two Olympic gold medals at the 2004 Athens Games in the 1,500 meters and the 5,000 meters. Guerrouj also won numerous gold medals at various world championships. For instance, he was the world record holder in the 1,500 meters at the 1998 world athletic championship. Additionally, he was named the International Association of Athletic Federations (IAAF) athlete of the year for 2000 and 2002. In the 1980s, his countryman, Said Aouita, dominated all middle-distance competitions. Aouita won a gold medal at the 1984 Los Angeles Olympic Games, and he was the overall winner of the IAAF Grand Prix series in 1985. In 1987, Aouita set world records in both the 2,000 meters and the 5,000 meters. Also at the 1984 Los Angeles Olympic Games, Nawal el Moutawakel, a world-class female runner, won a gold medal in the 400-meter hurdles. Her compatriot, Zahra Ouaziz, won a silver medal in the 5,000 meters at the 1999 World Championships. Perhaps it is not astonishing that Moroccans have been successful at middle-distance runs because both Guerrouj and Aouita were veterans of the challenging international Sand Marathon (or Marathon des Sables), arguably the most difficult marathon in the world. In tennis, Younes al Aynaoui, Karim Alami, and Hicham Arazi were once ranked among the top 100 on the world men's tennis circuit. Aynaoui, probably the most successful of all Moroccan tennis players, made it to the quarterfinals of the 2000 Australia Open.

Although there are other popular sports in Morocco, golf has serious patronage among Morocco's ruling elite. The late King Hassan II was widely known as a golfer, hence the wide popularity of the game. Many beautiful golf courses dot the country, such as that located at the Royal Dar as Salaam Golf Club in Rabat and Agadir. Three major international golf competitions are hosted in Morocco annually. These include the King Hassan II Trophy, the Moroccan Open, and the Mohammed VI Golf Trophy held at the Royal Dar as Salaam Golf Club.

Changing Leisure: Cinema

Morocco has always held a fascination for Western filmmakers, especially since the successful premiere of *Casablanca* in 1942. Going to movies is a popular pastime in this Muslim kingdom, and filmmaking is also a significant art. Hamid Bennani, whose film *Wechma* debuted in 1970, is widely acknowledged as the pioneer of contemporary Moroccan cinema. Prior to the 1970s, adaptations of Egyptian melodramas, which succeeded European films in the 1960s, dominated the popular cinema in the country. With the appearance of *Wechma* in theaters, however, a new film movement known as "cinematic modernity" began. The movement emphasized the ideas that cinema should be for more than entertainment purposes. It also represents an art, a way of thinking, a culture, a means of explaining reality, an intellectual pursuit, a form of writing based on signs, and using the environment and locations according to a new aesthetics. Cinematic modernity also aims to inform individuals about society and free them from superstitions, taboos, and authoritarian leadership. In this context, the filmmaker becomes "an intellectual, as well as an observer of his political and historical time."[5] These ideas inspired a number of impressive films produced in the 1970s and early 1980s, including Souheil Ben Barka's *A Thousand and One Hands (Mains mille et une)*, Moumen Smihi's *El Chergui*, Ahmed El Mamouni's *Days and Days (Des Jours et des jours)*, Hamed Bouani's *The Mirage (Le Mirage)*, Jillali Ferhati's *Les Poupees de Roseau*, Abderhamane Tazi's *Badis*, and Daoud Aoulad-Syad's *The Horse of Wind (Le Cheval de vent).*[6] In 1987, the government recognized the film industry as a potential source of revenue with the establishment of the National Institute of Drama, Art and Cultural Entertainment (NIDACE) as the agency responsible for the promotion of the industry.

Today, Moroccan cinema is breaking new ground as it continues to dramatize the social and political ills confronting the nation. Its ability to sustain a wider interest is anchored in the use of popular genres to depict current social problems. For instance, Saad Chraibi's *Women and Women (Femmes . . . et Femmes)*, a melodrama about women's rights activism, has enjoyed great success in Morocco. Similarly, Abdelkader Lagtaa's *Casablanca (Les Casablancais)* depicts modern Morocco's cities (particularly Casablanca) as places where people live in fear. The film portrays religious fundamentalism and political uncertainty as the principal sources of instability in society. Nabil Ayouch's *Mektoub* captures the wide gap between the rich and poor by focusing on the crime and conflict that poverty generates in society.

Although foreign films are also enjoyed by cinemagoers, those produced within the local cultural milieu particularly hold the most attraction for the people. Nonetheless, since the late 1990s, Morocco has become a hosting ground for popular film festivals. Among others, the annual Marrakech Film Festival (FIFM), usually held in December, attracts interest from Europe, the Americas, Africa, Asia, and the Middle East. The goal of the festival is both to celebrate the films of the previous years and to introduce new talent to the fast-growing industry. The FIFM affords foreign-based Moroccan filmmakers the opportunity to sample the success of their works at home. For instance, Hakim Belabbes's film *The Threads* is catching the interest of local film critics for it touch of realism.

OLD AND NEW: VILLAGES AND CITIES

Contemporary Morocco is a contrasting paradox of the old and new, village life and city life, poor and rich, and educated and uneducated. Also, although the country was introduced to the international capitalist system and modern professional careers under French and Spanish colonial tutelage, the precolonial pursuits of pastoralism, farming, hunting, pottery, and other crafts are still very much part of everyday life. As the succeeding governments continue to make significant efforts to modernize and improve agricultural production in the kingdom, this sector of the economy has remained in the hands of the rural farmers. The Berbers of the Atlas region and the Tuaregs of the south are primarily cattle herdsmen or pastoralists and move from place to place. In the rural areas, living conditions vary a great deal. Whereas the nomadic herdsmen often live in tents made of wool or goatskin, some farmers have their own houses. Generally the house is narrow and built in a more traditional manner, of stone or clay. Herdsmen are regulated to a lower status on the social hierarchy.

Those who opt to live a European lifestyle are found mostly in the big cities such as Rabat, Fès, Casablanca, and Meknès. Urban life presents a contrasting view of old and new residential quarters. Whereas the older and more conservative people live primarily in the old quarters (old medina), the younger middle-class and successful business and political elite tend to occupy the more modern buildings and quarters (new medina). The elite are also known for their conspicuous consumption and lifestyles, including expensive cars, palatial homes, expensive clothes and jewelry, and expensive foods and drinks.

Unlike in the past, it is fairly common to find young people at casinos, nightclubs, bars, and restaurants. In such towns as Marrakech and Agadir, modern nightclubs—some featuring erotic belly dancers—coexist alongside traditional modes of musical entertainment, such as folk dancing. These contrasting lifestyles express the continuing dynamics of social reordering going on in modern Morocco.

Agencies of Change

Given its strategic location between continents and cultures, Morocco has always been a dynamic society with cross-fertilization of cultural ideas and sociopolitical changes. European colonialism during the twentieth century, however, left a lasting legacy in the people's history. In the first four decades of the century, the impact of the various agencies of change, such as Western-style education, cash economy, modern bureaucracy, new technologies, infrastructures such as roads and railways, modern cities, hospitals, and so on, was kept at the best possible level within the terms of the Fès Treaty of 1912 that established French colonial rule. Toward the end of World War II, however, the Western presence produced a more pronounced and dramatic process of change in Morocco. Those living in the countryside began to migrate to the big cities in search of new opportunities and a better quality of life. Not everyone who migrated realized their dreams, but a good number of them were engaged in the new war economy. The development of port facilities during the war, for instance, led to the creation of new employment opportunities, especially in the coastal cities. The founding of light industries such as textile and sugar mills, tobacco factories, and food-processing plants provided additional opportunities for young people. These modest expansions in the industrial and service sectors of the economy were not enough to meet the needs of increasing numbers of the unemployed, however. In the late 1950s when Morocco attained its independence, about 80 percent of the population lived in rural areas, but the figure in the early 1980s decreased to 56 percent. An impressive study on literacy, culture, and development concluded in the 1990s showed that although the desire for Western-style education was increasing over this period, there were not enough educated people to meet the demands of the changing economic structures.[7] As a result of unemployment, several thousand were left to live in the misery of shantytowns, with an unsteady income, hunger, and poverty. In the midst of the unfortunates were successful businessman, entrepreneurs, and landowners living in palatial homes and luxurious apartments. Since independence, the governments have continued to search for a solution to the problems of unemployment, squalor, and illiteracy by creating more employment, expanding educational facilities, and creating new affordable housing options, especially in cities such as Casablanca and Rabat. The increasing population of young people and declining sources of revenue, however, have played a part in limiting the government's capacity to completely resolve these persistent issues.

Changing Economy and Values

As the economy continues to undergo a process of liberalization and modernization, so, too, do old values held by the people. On the economic front, privatization of state-owned companies began in earnest in 1993, and in the first four years, 34 government-owned companies were sold to the public, including banks, hotels, transport, and mining. Given that Moroccans purchased most of these companies, the middle class expanded and the number of shareholders jumped astronomically from 10,000 in 1993 to 180,000 in 1995. Additionally, foreign investments contributed nearly DH 4 billion (about U.S.$476.6 million) to the economy by 1995.[8] Although this initial opening in the economic sector continues to widen with a genuine support of the king, it leaves much to be desired. The much-expected privatization of the state-owned communication industry, for instance, is yet to be realized.

With regard to gender relations, Moroccan women are gradually experiencing a little more freedom and liberty as stipulated by Article 8 of the 1996 constitution. An observer of the recent changes noted that in the 1960s and 1970s, very few women had any role in politics because gender issues were considered secondary by the conservative male ruling elite.[9] This attitude is beginning to change, and Moroccans are steadily dropping some old customs and values. Since the 1980s, women have gained more power through emerging opportunities to pursue careers in government, academics, law, medicine, and other fields. Among prominent positions recently held by women, Nawal el-Moutawakel, who won the gold medal in the 400-meter hurdles at the 1984 Olympic Games, served as secretary of State for youth and sports between 1997 and 1998. In contrast to practices in the past, the younger and more educated generation has increasingly turned its back on polygamy and adopted tastes for university education, desire for employment in government service, fascination with European fashion, memberships in social clubs, and patronage of nightclubs and massage parlors. In the past, these lifestyle options were virtually intolerable in the society, but now the government is easing restrictions. Although large families are still desired by a significant portion of the population, the educated elite is increasingly opting for smaller and more manageable family sizes.

Changing Political Culture

In many ways, the recent socioeconomic changes on both the local and the global levels have also brought about new political pressures, thereby necessitating some changes in national politics and state structure. Since the late 1990s, when King Mohammed VI (who is seen primarily as a liberal) succeeded his father in office, the country has been going through a period of liberalization of state institutions. In fact, the political changes were part of the broader liberalizations King Hassan II had initiated before his death in July 1999. After repeated attempts on his life in the 1960s, 1970s, and 1980s by disgruntled elements in the country, in 1997 Hassan allowed elections for the House of Representatives for the first time in the country's history. Building on his father's example, in 2002 King Mohammed VI appointed a prime minister, Driss Jettou, to run the day-to-day affairs of government. Jettou was nonetheless under monarchical authority . In the 2002 election, more than 26 political parties vied for election. This was a promising effort by the government to get the people involved in the political process, but more are desired on the road to democratization as the new generation eagerly looks forward to a democratic government. This desire is best demonstrated by the sudden surge in the number of civil and political associations such as the Democratic Confederation of Labor (Confédération démocratique de travail, CDT), General Union of Moroccan Workers (Union Général des ouvriers marocains, UGTM), Moroccan Employers Association (Association Marocaine D'Employeurs, CGEM), National Labor Union of Morocco (Syndicat national du Maroc, UNMT), and Union of Moroccan Workers (Union des ouvriers marocains, UMT). These emergent groups may continue to apply pressure that will eventually bring about a full-blown democracy in Morocco. As an expert on Islamic societies stresses, "extremism flourishes in the absence of democracy."[10] In an age of international terrorism, democracy and human rights have crucial roles to play in curbing the rising tide of sectional cleavages and youthful radicalism in Morocco.

NOTES

1. Carolyn Fluehr-Lobban, *Islamic Societies in Practice,* 2nd ed. (Gainesville: University Press of Florida, 2004), 112.

2. Dale F. Eickelman, *Moroccan Islam: Tradition and Society in a Pilgrimage Center* (Austin: University of Texas Press, 1976), 158.

3. Ramadan may be literally translated as "the hot month."

4. The Berber founders of the Sa'adi dynasty took control of the southern part of Morocco from the Portuguese under their leader Mohammed Al Mahdi around 1550. In 1551, the leaders proceeded to take power in Morocco, making Marrakech their seat. It was during this period that the Badi palace, which was then one of the most exquisite architectural designs in history, was built. For details, see E. W. Bovill, *The Golden Trade of the Moors* (Oxford: Oxford University Press, 1968), 167–168.

5. See Hamadi Gueroum, "History of Moroccan Cinema," excerpts from the program of the 24th Festival of the 3 Continents, Nantes, France, November 24 through December 5, 2002.

6. For a recent discussion of these films, see Kevin Dwyer, *Beyond Casablanca: M. A. Tazi, Moroccan Cinema, and Third World Filmmaking* (Bloomington: Indiana University Press, 2004).

7. See Daniel A. Wagner, *Literacy, Culture, and Development: Becoming Literate in Morocco* (New York: Cambridge University Press, 1993).

8. C. R. Pennell, *Morocco since 1830: A History* (New York: New York University Press, 2000), 373–74.

9. C. R. Pennell, *Morocco since 1830: A History* (New York: New York University Press, 2000), 348.

10. Fluehr-Lobban, *Islamic Societies in Practice,* 7.

8

Music and Dance

UNLIKE IN MOST CONSERVATIVE Islamic states in Asia and the Middle East, in Morocco, music, which is often accompanied by dance, is central to everyday life and inseparable from the context in which it is performed. Music provides a medium for cultural, historical, and aesthetic expressions. Music also serves as a source of relaxation and entertainment. No festival or celebration is complete without music and dance, and certain kinds of African music can be seen as "communal property whose spiritual qualities are experienced and shared by all."[1] Musical groups entertain guests at birth, circumcision, and wedding parties and at concerts; provide pleasant distractions to mourners at funerals; and enliven religious processions. Like other Moroccan traditions, Moroccan music and dance reflect a rich mixture of Berber, Arab, Jewish, African, and European elements. This diversity underscores the enduring historical adaptation of the indigenous and foreign genres of popular culture.

In broad terms, experts have identified two types of Moroccan music: the various indigenous Berber varieties of music and performances that accompany traditional rituals, community entertainment, religious or a social observance, or recreational events such as sporting competitions and the classical music that predominates in the northern regions of Tangier, Tétouan, Fès, Meknès, Kenitra, and Rabat. The origin of Moroccan music goes back to the Andalusian period, the era beginning with the Arab conquest and rule of southern Spain in the early eight century and lasting until the Arab expulsion from Europe in the late fifteenth century (c. 711–1492).[2] Although this bipolar categorization provides a convenient analytical framework, it hardly explains the cross-fertilized and multidimensional nature of Moroccan music.

This chapter highlights the historical origins of the various genres, the types of performance, structural forms, repertoires, and events at which they are performed and how music and dance appear in the sociocultural milieu.

MUSICAL GENRES

The various genres of music and their recent adaptations may be understood in terms of their audience and uses. It is not uncommon to encounter individuals singing for a variety of reasons. One may sing to reduce boredom or loneliness or even to express love, joy, aspiration, expectation, hope, sorrow, or loss. Men and women sing to entertain their children, spouse, parents, and friends or to amuse themselves when they are engaged in various recreational, domestic, and vocational activities. The aggrieved may sing to bemoan a perceived act of injustice or to express hatred. A professional musician may, at the request of a patron, either perform as a soloist or in a group for the pleasure of a king, special guests, or other participants at a private party or banquet. Storytellers, circus performers, acrobats, and magicians at market places in Morocco use music and dance to capture the attention of their audience as they make a living. For each of these occasions, different kinds of musical instruments may be played. These may range from crude instruments such as sticks, empty cans, bottles, and hand clapping, to rattles, guitars, cymbals, piano, and drums.

The indigenous Berber culture is a repository of a variety of musical styles. Berber folk music and dance, which preceded the arrival of the Arabs in the late seventh century, accompany social ceremonies and rituals. They are performed by both nonprofessional and professional musicians (known as *imdyazn*) in a way that usually involves the entire village in a collective celebration of art and aesthetics. Some of the best-known contemporary Berber musicians include Walid Mimoun and Ammuri Mbark, whose band, the Usman, is recognized as transforming Berber song without losing its authentic and original appeal. Of no less importance are the all-male Master Musicians from the town of Jajouka, whose brand of traditional music has attracted immense interest among the Berber-Arabs. As a marker of community membership, Berber music allows people to dramatically and emotively express their feelings according to certain prescribed forms of behavior. Among the Berbers, music and dance serve as mediums for expressing forms of indigenous artistic, social, political, religious, and intellectual traditions and values, which also reveal adaptations from African ideas.

The so-called classical music of Morocco (also found throughout North Africa) has its roots in Andalusian music nurtured in Seville, Granada, and Cordoba. This legacy is often attributed to the artistic creations of the legendary Baghdad native Hassan Ali Ben Nafi (best known as Ziriab or Zyriab), who fled his homeland in the ninth century to escape a malicious plot by his enemies. His artistic contribution, in spite of the centuries of adaptations in Andalusia and North Africa, has endured as a melting pot of international cultural elements, and the lyrics are in either classical Arabic or in the Andalusian tongue (Gharnati). The multifaceted songs (including religious and secular tunes) associated with this genre use a wide variety of instruments such as the *tar* (or tambourine); a funnel-shaped drum made of clay called *darbuqa* or *darbouka;* three types of stringed instruments—the violin *(kemanjah),* fiddle *(rebab),* and lute *(oudh* or *oud*), which has a larger, pear-shaped body; and other modern instruments such as clarinets, banjos, and pianos. Lyrics for the classical melodies are written in the most stylish and scholarly form of Arabic. Future musicians receive extended training at music schools in Marrakech and Rabat.

Over the years, classical compositions have undergone extensive changes, including a simplified form of lyrics that use everyday Arabic to form a subgenre of the Andalusian original. The evolving variety is commonly known in Morocco as *griha.* Some experts have identified *griha* as part of the mainstream popular culture because it typically deals with widely appealing themes of everyday life such as crime, immorality, religious bigotry, poverty, women's issues, wars, and adventure.[3] The songs are accompanied by intricate dances. Generally, Moroccan folklore includes a variety of musical styles that serve as a repertoire of oral text. This form of artistic creation captures an aspect of the indigenous knowledge system and has also been adapted by some religious brotherhoods for ritual celebrations.

Music for Storytelling

Storytelling is an integral part of Berber life. Moroccan folklore is extremely diverse and varies from region to region. Each community—whether nomadic or sedentary—has its own rich supply of dramas, operas, musical works, specific skills, devices, and elements available for performance. Whether encountered in the indigenous (Berber), classical, or contemporary (modern) popular culture, the music is rich in historical accounts, legends, myths, heroic deeds, chronologies of dynasties and rulers, and important wars that inform the audience about values and the way people have lived. Whereas Adalusian music narrates the achievements or downfalls of the Moroccan people, its Berber equivalent uses the tambourine and reed flute to convey smooth-flowing stories in harmony with the percussion.[4] Music as a form of indigenous Berber culture has been preserved by small bands of itinerant professional entertainers who offer their songs, tales, and poetry in marketplaces, at weddings, births, circumcisions, and occasions for monetary rewards.

Argan music of southern Morocco is a popular folk music that celebrates the people's culture and reminds the younger generation about their indigenous values. The seeds of the *argania spinosa* tree, locally called *argan,* are edible, and dark oil is extracted for medicinal purposes. It grows around the southwestern towns of Essaouira and Agadir. For the local people of Souss (or Sus), Tamanar, Immouzer, and Inezgane, the tree symbolizes endurance and the will to survive in the challenging desert environment and represents an intricate aspect of being a Berber, hence it occupies a central part of the people's folklore and everyday social life. Among other things, *argan* performers sing about their cultural tradition, common issues in their immediate and neighboring environment, and the incursion of foreign influences on the social order. Although this tradition goes back in time, the folklore is constantly being enriched by popular ideas, and new songs are composed and revised to reflect recent events on the national, community, or individual level.

Another genre of music for storytelling is the *quasida,* which is a type of epic, a composition in the form of narrative verse, preserved in the local language. The music celebrates events of exceptional interest such as the joys or misfortunes that have befallen the nation or the achievements of famous individuals. The *quasida* is similar to the popular eighteenth- and nineteenth-century slow and sentimental English ballad.[5]

Music and Dance for War

Berbers have been known for their impressive and heroic achievements in battles, and traditional Moroccan music and dance include some genres that were originally performed in times of war. Examples include the *ahidni, ghiayta,* and *taskioine* dances. With the emergence of the modern state in Africa, such war songs and dances only exist as cultural remnants. Participants may include both the educated and uneducated, the religious and nonreligious, the rural and urban dwellers, and so on. In some communities, both men and women participate; in others, war dances are only for men. Traditionally, the men wore or carried such war paraphernalia as swords, knives, rifles, arrows, sharpened sticks, and amulets as they danced to a particular war song. Of the different types of this genre, the *ahidni* dance is the most celebrated. Dancers stand close to one another in a circle, and as they sing, they rhythmically clap their hands and stomp their feet in an aggressive and belligerent manner.

Similarly, the *ghiaytas* war dance serves to provide soldiers with courage in preparation for a war and embodies a form of victory celebration. During the dance, the warriors, holding their rifles, move their bodies in response to the tune of pipes and the beat of drums. The performers shout rather than sing.

They carry their rifles on their heads, mimic the movements of soldiers in real combat situations, and then pretend to shoot at enemies. Dancing in a circle, the performers aim their rifles to the ground, and at the command of their leader fire blank shots. Among the Haha people of the High Atlas region, a simple reed flute with seven-holes takes the melody, and the rhythm is made by clapping and stomping to give a commanding and enchanting effect. The male performers dance in an aggressive manner that shows masculine passion.

The *taskioine* is another traditional warriors' dance exclusively for men. Wearing white tunics and turbans, with powder horns on their shoulders, the dancers respond to the beat of earthenware tambourines covered with skins. They make well-rehearsed sudden stops with aggressive stamping of the feet. Although the *taskioine* dance is more of a physical activity than an artistic performance, the aesthetic values are nevertheless present.

Another traditional war dance involves acrobatic displays from the brotherhood of Sidi Ahmed ou Moussa (or Hmaid ou Moussa, the saint of Tazeroualt, from the Anti-Atlas Mountains), who established a training center for acrobats at the village of Amizmiz near Marrakech. Originally, the young people of the area performed these exercises in preparation for their role as sharpshooters and archers. As traditional warfare gradually declined with the emergence of the modern nation-state in Africa, the young acrobats of Tazeroualt turned the skills associated with this traditional dance into a moneymaking circus. Some of the dancers have taken their talents overseas as entertainers in Europe and the United States. In the diaspora, the traditional elegant costumes with colorful embroidery have been largely retained.

Religious and Ritual Music

Although some types of Berber and Andalusian music were originally composed for religious worship and ritual ceremonies, they also may be played during secular events. Like most spirituals, sacred tunes of Morocco are usually soft melodies. The mandolin and the violin are some of the common instruments used in this type of music. Singing and clapping often accompany these instruments. Also included among this genre is the Sephardic Jewish music of the diaspora. In Morocco, whereas the topical and entertaining songs of the Sephardim remain part of the popular culture, the spiritual tunes are an intricate part of religious and cultural celebrations among the Jewish communities of North Africa.

The original Berber spirituals have been adapted and changed since the coming and spread of Islam in the Maghreb, even though some still have not been accepted and modified by (orthodox) Islam. For instance, the *guedra* dance from the southern region of Morocco has its roots in the pre-Islamic

Berber religious practices. The *guedra* belongs to the so-called Blue People—the Tuaregs—of Goulimine, the region of the Sahara that stretches from the northern fringes of Mauritania all the way to Algeria and Egypt.[6] The *guedra* is, in fact, a type of local earthenware cooking pot that can be easily converted to a drum that produces a special sound. Stemming from their pervasive belief in the existence of spirits (djinns), the Berber women performers appear completely covered in a black costume that reveals only their heads as a precaution against fiendish attacks. As they kneel, the dancers move to a steady rhythm that conjures culture, drama, and aesthetics. The performance is total theater when dancers sing in their local dialect and the spectators respond with alternating ecstatic and brief guttural cries. To end the performance, the dancers cast aside their veils before they dramatically fall on the ground.

In the town of Tissint (or Tisint), which lies southward of Agadir in the Anti-Atlas region, men and women, completely dressed in indigo, perform a dance also known by the name *tissint,* which can be traced back to an indigenous religious rite. In this betrothal rite of passage, the use of daggers symbolizes persistence, pursuit, and victory. The engagement ceremony requires potential suitors and young women of marriageable age to meet and organize themselves in circle. The participants dance to a rhythmic, fast-tempo tune performed by locals and nonprofessionals who clap, chant, and sing with friends and acquaintances. The participants, including their watchful chaperones, guardians, and parents, sit in a circle, creating a dance space at the middle. One by one, a girl leaves the circle to dance. Soon, a suitor, who proposes to her by holding up a dagger fastened around his waist with a cord, joins her. The dagger represents an offer of protection and an indication of the intent to take up spousal responsibility for the woman. The young man spins, making circles around the girl, withdraws, and comes nearer, until they are facing each other. The official betrothal is observed as soon as the potential bride allows her suitor to put the corded belt over her head. With a deliberately slow movement, the man goes down on his knees in front of his future spouse. This custom has survived despite the fight by Islamic conservatives for its abolition. The *tissint* dance is among the original Berber folk dances that are favored by the Ministry of Culture for inclusion in the annual Marrakech Folk Festival. This official patronage has left the Tuaregs with the hope of retaining their cherished custom at least in the near future.

Music for Guilds

Certain genres of music are specifically produced by craftsmen's guilds. Among these are the *malhun* and *dekka* songs. Whereas the *malhun,* encountered primarily in poetry, is identified generally with the urban working class craftsmen's guilds, the *dekka* exclusively belongs to the craftsmen and merchants from Marrakech. The entertainers are not professional musicians. The instruments are different-sized earthenware drums. The ceremony starts with simple and rather solemn rhythms, then the tempo of clapping accelerates. The percussion is cleverly orchestrated, and the chorus of men sings powerfully. The rhythm changes now and then in a well-rehearsed manner, creating a response that manifests in a resounding outburst of ecstasy and excitement.

Musical Games

Other forms of music and dance in Morocco are made to entertain participants at traditional games and sporting competitions. This genre occupies a rightful place in the traditional folk music, which attracts tourists from far and wide. Among them is the familiar horse festival (or fantasia) of Meknès. One of the highlights of this exciting display of horsemanship is the music and dance session that brings the festival to a grand close. The participants are dressed in diverse and rich costumes, and the music style played reflects the rich tradition of the people.

Music for Entertainment and Recreation

Although all forms of music and dance entertain their audience, folk musicians and dancers have an ensemble of traditions that are specially put together for amusement and relaxation. A good example is the *awash* (or *ahwach*) dance that has become a major attraction at the annual June Marrakech Folk Festival. The skillful dancers from the High Atlas valleys in the Ouarzazate area appear in sparkling costumes. As in most Moroccan dances, the women form a circle and men sit around a fire at the center, each of them holding a circular wooden tambourine called a *bendir*. The performance commences with a piercing cry that is quickly followed by drumbeats. As the tempo increases, the women pick up the chorus, moving their bodies slowly and then faster as their shoulders touch until the final chorus.

The *ouais* is another popular music style for entertainment and recreation. It may be described as an adaptation of indigenous lyrics with English ballet and Arab culture. The instruments used are a one-stringed fiddle (*rebab* or *rbab soussi*) and a number of small mandolins (*guembris*) sometimes with three strings and made from a turtle shell. An instrumentalist who strikes a piece of cast iron lying on the ground provides the commanding rhythm. The dancers add to the music with small copper cymbals attached to their fingers. All the dancers wear city clothes, including a traditional caftan, an embroidered silk belt *(dfina),* and a cord adorned with beads woven around the head. The performers with their elegant steps create an uncommonly graceful spectacle.

The music and dance of the Gnawas (or Gnaouas) of the High Atlas are of black African and Arab traditions. It is a typical trance music used by members of the Sufi brotherhood to attain mystical ecstasy. Members of the group, who claim descent from Sidi Bilal, the ex-slave from Ethiopia who became a highly respected caller to prayers (muezzin), include master musicians, drummers, intriguing-looking women, mediums, and others who a long time ago established their home in Marrakech and other southern regions. The West African slaves who arrived in North Africa in the sixteenth century brought this genre to Morocco; consequently, the lyrics have components of Senegalese, Guinean, and Malian traditions. A lute *(qsbah)* with a long neck of African origin called the *gimbri,* double-iron cymbals *(qaraqab),* and a double-headed cylindrical drum *(tbel* or *ganga)* played with curved sticks are common instruments of the Gnawa music. Members of the brotherhood observe a nocturnal rite of ceremonious possession *(deiceba),* during which participants practice the dances of possession and trance called *derdeba.* A master musician accompanies his troupe, and a female medium usually leads the spirituals used to invocate saints and supernatural beings. The percussion for the ritual processions comes specifically from a lute drum with a low register *(guembri)* and castanets *(qraqech).* Drums are used only during the beginning stage preceding the rite of possession. This nighttime ceremony also includes an irreligious session intended solely for the entertainment of members. Today, the tumblers of the Jemaa El Fna (or Djema el-Fna) in Marrakech have transformed Gnawa music and dance into a popular form of entertainment. The group retains the traditional large drums and wrought-iron castanets and the cowry shells and glass beads that adorn the performers. These cultural emblems remind the people about the dance's historical origins. The Gnawa performers dance with much agility, and their dangerous acrobatics flow with the beat of the rhythm.

The *ahidou* is one of the most celebrated Middle Atlas arts and is performed by elegantly dressed dancers of the Oulmes and Khenifra areas. The men and women form a large circle and dance to the tempo of the local tambourine *(bendir).* Unlike the daring acrobats of the Gnawas, the *ahidou* performers dance with simple modesty and grace, and the songs have poetic lyrics. The women wear blue cloaks *(handiras)* with white stripes. Married women and widows may wear a kind of henna in their hair called *akidoud.* Their exquisite costumes are completed with large ornaments made of yellow amber beads and silver. The men dress in long traditional clothes called burnooses and wear headgear or turbans. The *ahidou* concert is enthralling, and the dignified gestures have endured as the trademark of this group.

The *houara* dancers of Inezgane are troupes made up of local men and one woman. It represents one of the most fantastic types of folk dancing of Morocco. In readiness for the ceremony that is deeply laden with sacred and secular meaning, the dancers and singers organize themselves in a circle with the men and the woman standing close to one another. The rhythm is produced with tambourines, and the performers sing cheerily to both spiritual and sacred songs. The men leave the circle alone or in pairs to dance. As the tempo of the music reaches a certain speed, the woman rushes to the center to join the men in the dance. The dances involve a lot of physical activity and elaborate steps.

The *shikhat* are female singing groups whose performances have become a crucial part of most festive celebrations and private parties in Morocco. They entertain guests at marriage ceremonies, henna parties, and birth and circumcision celebrations. A troupe of performers is typically made up of three or four women and a couple of male members who play only a supporting role. Whereas the men play an assortment of small drums (the *darbuka,* the *taarija,* the *bendir*), the women sing, dance, and sometimes drum their feet on an overturned metal washbasin *(aj-jafna).* The male members of the troupe, numbering usually no more than three, are responsible for playing heavy instruments such as the fiddle *(kamanja),* drums, and a three-stringed small-bodied instrument known locally as the *lotar.* In a society where women are customarily expected to be modest in their behavior, the *shikhat* is considered by most committed Muslims as a risqué form of entertainment because of the erotic movements of the dancers. A detailed study of the *shikhat* in Morocco reveals that although the female performers are widely perceived as an aberration of the ideal woman, they nonetheless represent the inner thoughts of the so-called "honorable women insofar as they are licensed in the performance context to publicize the private desires and disappointments of the majority of Moroccan women."[7] The performers fulfill this role not only by revealing women's private life in public celebrations but also by doing it in a vulgar manner. This form of performance can be seen an act of defiance in a society in which masculine power is paramount. To "express sexuality is … an act of defiance."[8]

Pop Music

Popular music, or *chaabi* (Arabic for "popular"), traditionally performed in marketplaces in Morocco, encompasses diverse forms. It draws on many aspects of local, African, Arab, and Western styles, and the language of communication is mostly colloquial Arabic or Moroccan Arabic, widely spoken or understood by all. The modern form of the pop music evolved in the 1970s with the appearance of Nass El Ghiwane, JilJilala, Lem Chaheb, and Noujoum Ouazza as the stars of the new music generation. Among the most successful of the emergent artists is Ouazza, a talented singer and guitarist who played for a band called Lem Chaheb. He is credited with producing the most appealing lyrics of the North African pop music dominant in the 1970s and 1980s. Most of the pop songs have an instrumental section *(leseb)* that allows the audience to join in singing and clapping. The music is produced with instruments ranging from indigenous ones such as lute and drum to modern ones such as the piano and electric guitar. Whereas Lem Chaheb and El Ghiwane have made themselves enemies of the government because of the intense political nature of their songs, Najat Aatabou, who rose to stardom with her album entitled *Country Girls and City Women,* is gaining popularity with her more nuanced comments on the erosion of family values and religious hypocrisy in society.

Also among the contemporary North African music styles is *rai,* which originated in western Algeria but has wide appeal in Morocco. It can be best described as an amalgam of local and other Arab, African, and European styles. This eclecticism is best heard in the music of Mustafa Loumghari, who spent more than a decade of his life in the Netherlands. His debut album, *Noujoum Amsterdam,* was an instant success at private parties, social events, and on national radio. His subsequent album, *The Mediterranean (Le Méditerranéen),* which he dedicated to the children of the world, further captured the intricate mix of multicultural lyrics in *rai* music.

Other Hybrids and Music from Other Lands

Although Western music is gradually making its entrance via foreign radio stations and satellite television, and young people patronize clubs owned by Westerners and local entrepreneurs, mainstream Western music, such as rap and hip-hop, has yet to gain a wide audience in this Muslim country. Other music from around the world is widely enjoyed in Morocco, however. A variety of sacred music is featured at the annual international Fès Festival of World Sacred Music. This festival attracts top sacred music artists from Europe, the United States, Africa, the Middle East, and other parts of Asia for a week of exhibitions and concerts. Hindu chants, Christian gospel songs, Sufi dervishes from Turkey and Uzbekistan, and Celtic chants are some of the most popular performances at the festival. These foreign spirituals are joined by the rich flavors of Berber trance music and Arab-Adalusian and Sephardic spirituals in an enchanting mix of arts and cultural traditions. This celebration of music is also very popular among the ruling elite in Morocco.

Other brands of foreign music found in Morocco include jazz and Egyptian music, although jazz is not popular. Jazz and Egyptian music have roots in Africa, and they represent other examples of foreign music that are gradually attracting popular patronage. Whereas jazz appeals to a medium-sized audience, Egyptian music, which attracts a larger audience, may be described as part of the diverse terrain of popular music found within the Arab-Berber North African social milieu.

NOTES

1. See W. Komla Amoaku, "Towards a Definition of Traditional African Music: A Look at the Ewe of Ghana," in Irene V. Jackson, ed., *More Than Drumming* (Westport, CT: Greenwood, 1985), 32.

2. Andalusia is the Arabic word for Spain; hence, the term *Andalusian* denotes the era of Arab conquest and control of parts of Spanish land.

3. See, for instance, Harold D. Nelson, ed., *Morocco: A Country Study,* 4th ed. (Washington, D.C.: American University Press, 1978), 140–141. See also Eugene Fodor and William Curtis, *Fodor's Morocco 1973* (New York: David McKay, 1973), 110–113.

4. Fodor and Curtis, *Fodor's Morocco,* 111–112.

5. Ibid., 112.

6. The Tuaregs are called the "Blue People" because of their use of indigo to color pieces of fabric. The deeper the color in the fabric, the more beautiful they consider the item of clothing and the higher the status of the wearer, because more was spent to get the richer color.

7. Deborah A. Kapchan, "Moroccan Female Performers Defining the Social Body," *Journal of American Folklore* 107, no. 423 (winter 1994): 89.

8. Lila Abu-Lughod, *Veiled Sentiments: Honor and Poetry in a Bedouin Society* (Berkeley: University of California Press, 1986), 157.

Glossary

aith.   Berber word for "sons of."

alem (singular, *oulem* or *alim*).   Pious scholars of the premodern Middle East.

al-haja.   Title for Muslim women who have performed the pilgrimage to Mecca.

al-haji.   Title for Muslim men who have performed the pilgrimage to Mecca.

Allah.   One and only God.

Amaziah (or *imazighan*).   Literally "free men"; the original name by which the Berber people of North Africa identified themselves.

baraka.   Sign of divine favor, sanctity, or special blessing from God (Allah), an attribute of holy men and saints of Morocco.

Barbarus.   Name by which the ancient Romans referred to the indigenous inhabitants of North Africa.

ben (or bin).   Arabic for "son of."

besiff.   Arabic for "sword."

bidonville.   Shantytown or slum neighboring a cosmopolitan area, often created by poor immigrants.

bled-el-makhzen.   Part of Morocco under the control of the sultan.

bled-el-siba.   Part of Moroccan land not firmly under the control of the sultan.

Blue Men.   Common name for Berber Tuaregs because of their gorgeous blue robes and tradition of body painting with indigo.

burnoose.   Hooded woolen cloak originally for men.

caliph.   Originally a successor to the Prophet Muhammad, but now one who rules a Muslim state.

Casbah.   Palace or fortress.

chaabi.   Arabic for "popular."

colon.   French colonial settler in Morocco.

dayyanim.   Jewish rabbi-judge in Morocco.

dfoua.   Arabic for "bridewealth or dowry."

dhimmis.   Literally "protected people"; generic term for non-Muslims, especially Christians and Jews living in predominantly Muslim societies.

dirham (DH).   Unit of currency in Morocco; as of May 7, 2005, U.S.$1 = DH 8.67320.

djellaba (or *zellaba*).   Short, hooded woolen cloak with wide sleeves for men.

djinn (or jinn).   Invisible spirits, including both benevolent and malevolent, believed to be everywhere among the living.

guembri.   Small mandolin with three strings sometimes made from a turtle shell. Some are a carved wooden piece covered with animal skin like a drum.

hakawati.   Arabic term for itinerant actors and entertainers, including storytellers, acrobats, magicians, snake charmers, dancers, and preachers.

Hegira *(hejra).*   Flight of the Prophet Muhammad from Mecca to Medina in 622 c.e. following plans by his local leaders to kill him.

henna.   Dye of reddish brown color obtained from the henna plant; used prominently in Berber culture for body painting, especially during marriage and other ceremonies.

iblis.   Satan or chief of the malevolent spirits or demons.

ihram.   Seamless white garment often worn by male pilgrims at the holy sites in Mecca but also won by others in all Islamic countries.

Imam.   Generally, a leader of prayer or a spiritual leader.

imdyazn.   Berber for a professional musician.

Istiqlal.   Independence.

jihad.   Struggle or striving in defense of Islam; when this struggle assumes a violent dimension, it becomes a holy war, and such warriors are known as *mujahids.*

Ka'aba.   Small stone building in the court of the Great Mosque at Mecca that holds the black stone given to Abraham by the Angel Gabriel; it represents the "holy of holies" in Islam and lies at the heart of the annual pilgrimage (hajj) ceremonies.

kemanjah.   Violin.

ksar.   Fortified section of the **Casbah** where loyal residents sought protection in the era of the Islamic invasions of North Africa and Spain; however, in the Sahara and Atlas Mountain regions, the word generally connotes fortified and walled villages.

madrassa.   School or college for Islamic education, often attached to a mosque.

Maghreb.   Arabic for "further west"; now denotes the region occupied by Morocco, Algeria, and Tunisia.

mahr.   Arabic term for "dowry."

Marabout.   Islamic holy man, especially belonging to the Sufi religious order, teaching at local levels.

masjid.   Arabic for "mosque," the Muslim place for public worship.

mdemma.   Waist belt made of superior leather and fixed with satin strips and gold embroidery.

medina.   Arabic for "town"; indicates the original Arab quarters in Moroccan towns.

mellah (or *mallah*).   Old Jewish residential quarters in Moroccan towns.

Moores.   Designation from which the name Morocco is derived.

mousseums.   Arabic for "festivals," especially the various religious and secular festivals in honor of a saint.

objets d'envoi.   French expression for prestigious objects that can serve as a dignified image of its country of origin.

oudh (**or oud;** Arabic *qsbah*).   Traditional lute.

qadi.   Muslim judge or administrator of justice.

qaid.   Local chief or district administrator.

qaraqab.   Double iron cymbals.

Quarish (or Quraysh).   The Prophet Muhammad's kinsmen, the family of Mecca.

Quran.   Islam's holy scripture (or "recitation") as revealed to the Prophet Muhammad.

rai.   Form of popular music in North Africa, best described as an amalgam of local and other varieties of Arab, African, and European styles.

Ramadan.   The ninth month of the Islamic lunar calendar, during which Muslims observe a thirty-day fasting period, one of the five pillars of Islam.

rebab (or *rbab soussi*).   One-stringed fiddle.

ribat.   Pledge or pact.

salaam.   "Peace," and also a common greeting among Muslims.

salat.   Prescribed ritual prayer observed five times a day and one of the five pillars of Islam.

sawn.   Act of fasting and one of the five pillars in Islam; usually associated with Ramadan.

Sephardi (plural, Sephardim).   Ancestors of modern Moroccan Jews who arrived from Spain.

shahadah.   Article of faith, or "witness," and one of the five pillars of Islam affirming that "there is no god but God, and Mohammed is the Prophet of God."

sharia.   Islamic code of civil and criminal law derived from the Quran and the Prophet Muhammad's teachings and examples.

sharif (plural, *shurfa*).   Descendants of the holy lineage who trace descent from the Prophet Muhammad.

Shiites.   Sect in Islam that shares the understanding that Ali, the son-in-law of the Prophet Muhammad, should be the successor to the Prophet.

shor (or *s'hur*).   Arabic for "witchcraft."

souk.   Market often specializing in a product in the medina.

Sufi.   Order of the mystical dimension of Islam; especially a believer who deemphasizes material pursuits for direct spiritual encounter with God.

Sunna.   Tradition and custom of Mohammed; second in authority only to the Quran.

Sunni.   One who adheres to the traditions of the Prophet of Allah.

sura.   Chapter of the Quran.

taarija.   Tambourine.

ulema.   Community of learned Islamic men.

umma.   Community of believers.

vizier.   Highly ranked executive officer, often a provincial leader, in various Muslim countries.

waqf.   Special charitable gifts bequeathed in the form of endowments and dedicated in honor of God.

zakat (or *sadaqa*).   Almsgiving to the poor and the needy by Muslims; one of the five pillars of Islam.

zelliges.   Ceramic tiles.

Bibliographic Essay

THERE ARE MANY BOOKS, essays, and monographs on the various subjects discussed in this book. Some are published in Morocco; others are printed outside the country. A good deal of these texts are published in English; however, the bulk of other materials is in French and Arabic and are therefore not always accessible to the English readers. I have included only a few of the most important secondary sources used.

GENERAL

Some of the various materials referenced on the culture and customs of the Middle East and Africa in general and Morocco in particular are Harvey E. Goldberg, ed., *Sephardi and Middle Eastern Jewries: History and Culture in the Modern Era* (Bloomington: Indiana University Press, 1996); I. William Zartman, ed., *Man, State, and Society in the Contemporary Maghrib* (New York: Praeger, 1973); Carolyn Fluerhr-Lobban, *Islamic Societies in Practice,* 2nd ed. (Gainesville: University Press of Florida, 2004); Masudul Alam Choudhury, *The Islamic Worldview: Socio-Scientific Perspectives* (New York: Keegan Paul, 2000); Claudia Roden, *A Book on Middle Eastern Food* (New York: Knopf, 1972); Valérie K. Orlando, *Of Suffocated Hearts and Tortured Souls: Seeking Subjecthood through Madness in Francophone Women Writing of Africa and Caribbean* (Lanham, MD: Lexington Books, 2003); C. R. Pennell, *Morocco since 1830: A History* (New York: New York University Press, 2000); Rafic Boustani and Philippe Fargues, *The Atlas of the Arab World Geopolitics and Society* (New York: Facts on File, 1991); Mervyn Hiskett, *The Course of Islam in Africa* (Edinburgh: Edinburgh

University Press, 1994); Michael Brett, ed., *North Africa: Islam and Modernization* (London: Frank Cass, 1973); Stephane Bernard, *The Franco-Moroccan Conflict* (New Haven, CT: Yale University Press, 1968); Ernest Gellner and Charles Micaud, eds., *Arabs and Berbers: From Tribe to Nation in North Africa* (Lexington, Massachusetts: Lexington Books, 1972); William A. Hoisington Jr., *Lyautey and the French Conquest of Morocco* (New York: St. Martin's, 1995).

INTRODUCTION

For information on the history and other facts of Morocco, see the following: Dale F. Eickelman, *Moroccan Islam: Tradition and Society in a Pilgrimage Center* (Austin: University of Texas Press, 1976); American University Foreign Area Studies Division (FASD), *Area Handbook for Morocco* (Washington, D.C.: U.S. Government Printing Office, 1966); V. C. Scott O'Connor, *A Vision of Morocco* (Garden City, NY: Doubleday, Page and Company, 1924); Harold D. Nelson, ed., *Morocco: A Country Study* (Washington, D.C.: American University Press, 1985); Wayne Edge, *Global Studies: Africa,* 11th ed. (Dubuque, IA: McGraw-Hill, 2006); Abdeslam M. Maghraoui, "Depolitization in the Arab World? Depolitization in Morocco, *Journal of Democracy* 13, no. 4 (October 2002): 25–32; Jean-Francois and James Paul, "Morocco's Bourgeoisie: Monarchy, State and Owing Class," *MERIP Middle Eastern Report* 142 (September–October 1983): 13–17; Clement Eleanor Hoffmann, *Realm of the Evening Star: A History of Morocco and the Land of the Moors* (Philadelphia: Chilton Books, 1965); Pierre Parent, *The Truth about Morocco,* trans. Eleanor Knight (Flushing, NY: Moroccan Office of Information and Documentation, 1953); C. R. Pennell, *Morocco: From Empire to Independence* (Oxford, UK: One World, 2003); Mark I. Cohen and Hahn Lorna, *Morocco: Old Land, New Nation* (New York: Praeger, 1966); Frank H. Braun, "Morocco: Anatomy of a Palace Revolution that Failed," *International Journal of Middle East Studies* 9 (1978): 63–72; Uriel Dann, *King Hussein and the Challenge of Arab Radicalism: Jordan, 1955–1967* (New York: Oxford University Press in cooperation with the Moshe Dayan Center for Middle Eastern and African Studies, Tel Aviv University, 1989); Paul Bowles, *Morocco—Sahara to the Sea* (New York: Abbeville Press, 1995); Annette Solyst, *Timeless Places—Morocco* (New York: Friedman/Fairfax, 2000); David Hart, *Banditry in Islam: Case Studies from Morocco, Algeria and Pakistan North West Frontier* (Wisbech, UK: Middle East and North African Studies, 1987); Julia Clancy-Smith, ed., *North Africa, Islam, and the Mediterranean World: From Almoravids to the Algerian War* (Portland, OR: Frank Cass, 2001).

Religion and Worldview

On indigenous religion, Islam, and cosmology, the following works were consulted: Ira G. Zepp Jr., *A Muslim Primer: Beginner's Guide to Islam*, 2nd ed. (Fayetteville: University of Arkansas Press, 2000); Carolyn Fluehr-Lobban, *Islamic Societies in Practice*, 2nd ed. (Gainesville: University Press of Florida, 2004); Mervyns Hiskett, *The Course of Islam in Africa* (Edinburgh: Edinburgh University Press, 1994); Edward Westermarck, *The Belief in Spirits in Morocco* (Abo, Finland: Abo Akademi Press, 1920); M. W. Hilton-Simpson, "Some Superstitions Noted among the Shawia Berbers of the Auries Mountains and Their Nomad Neighbors, *Folklore* 26 (1915): 228–234; Roger Joseph and Terri Brint Joseph, *The Rose and the Thorn: Semiotic Structures in Morocco* (Tucson: University of Arizona Press, 1987); David Montgomery Hart, *The Aith Waryaghar of the Moroccan Rif: An Ethnography and History* (Tucson: University of Arizona Press, 1978); Richard F. Nyrop et al., *Area Handbook for Morocco* (Washington, D.C.: U.S. Government Printing Press, 1972); Clifford Geertz, *Islam Observed: Religious Development in Morocco and Indonesia* (New Haven, CT: Yale University Press, 1968); Abdellah Hammoudi, *The Victim and Its Masks: An Essay on Sacrifice and Masquerade in the Maghreb*, trans. Paula Wissing (Chicago: University of Chicago Press, 1993). For religion and power in Morocco, the following were consulted: John P. Entelis, ed., *Islam, Democracy and the State in North Africa* (Bloomington: Indiana University Press, 1997); Rahma Bourqia and Susan Gilson Miller, eds., *In the Shadow of the Sultan: Culture, Power, and Politics in Morocco* (Cambridge, MA: Harvard University Press, 1999); I. William Zartman, *Morocco: Problems of a New Power* (New York: Atherton Press, 1964); David Robinson, *Muslim Societies in African History* (New York: Cambridge University Press, 2002); H. Byron Earhart, ed., *Religious Traditions of the World: A Journey through Africa, Mesoamerica, North America, Judaism, Christianity, Islam, Hinduism, Buddhism, China, and Japan* (San Francisco: Harper, 1993); John Ruedy, ed., *Islam and Secularism in North Africa* (New York: St. Martin's Press, 1994).

Literature and Media

Valérie K. Orlando, *Nomadic Voices of Exile: Feminine Identity in Francophone Literature of the Maghreb* (Athens: Ohio University Press, 1999); Winifred Woodhull, *Transfigurations of the Maghreb: Feminism, Decolonization, and Literatures* (Minneapolis: University of Minnesota Press, 1993); Andreas Flores Khalil, *The Arab Avant-Garde: Experiments in North African Literature* (Westport, CT: Praeger, 2003); Mohammed Abu-Talib, "Drink to the Prophet," in Richard S. Harrel, William S. Caroll, and Mohammed Abu-Talib, eds., *A Basic Course in Moroccan Arabic* (Washington, D.C.: Georgetown University Press, 2003); Paul Bowles, *A Study of the Short Fiction* (New York: Allen Hibbard, 1993); Roger Allen, *The Arabic Literary Heritage: The Developments of Its Genres and Criticism* (Cambridge: Cambridge University Press, 1998); Arthur Palmer Hudson, *Folklore Keeps the Past Alive* (Athens: University of Georgia Press, 1962); Zohra Mezgueldi, "Mother-word and French-Language in Moroccan Writing," *Research in African Literatures* 27, no. 3 (fall 1996): 1–14; Heidi Abdel-Jaouad, "'Too Much in the Sons': Mothers and Impossible Alliances in Francophone Maghrebian Writing," *Research in African Literatures* 27, no. 3 (fall 1996): 15–33; Elias Canetti, *The Voices of Marrakesh: A Record of a Visit,* trans. J. A. Underwood (New York: Seabury Press, 1978); Norman A. Stillman, *The Language and Culture of the Jews of Sefrou, Morocco: An Ethnolinguistic Study* (Manchester, UK: University of Manchester Press, 1988); Henry Munson Jr., *Religion and Power in Morocco* (New Haven, CT: Yale University Press, 1993); Harold D. Nelson, ed., *Morocco: A Country Study,* 4th ed. (Washington, D.C.: American University Press, 1978); Edward Westermarck, *The Belief in Spirits in Morocco* (Abo, Finland: Abo Akademi Press, 1920); Edward Westermarck, *Ritual and Belief in Morocco* (London: n.p., 1926); Edward Westermarck, *Wit and Wisdom in Morocco: A Study of Native Proverbs* (London: Routledge, 1930); Ernest Gellner, *Saints of the Atlas* (Chicago: University of Chicago Press, 1969); Roger Le Tourneau, *Fez in the Age of the Marinides,* trans. Besse Alberta Clement (Norman: University of Oklahoma Press, 1961); Roger Joseph and Terri Brint Joseph, *The Rose and the Thorn: Semiotic Structures in Morocco* (Tucson: University of Arizona Press, 1987); Said Hamdun and Noel King, *Ibn Battuta in Black Africa* (Princeton, NJ: Markus Wiener, 1996); Mahdi Agha Husain, "Manuscripts of Ibn Battuta's Rihla in Paris," *Journal of the Asiatic Society of Bengal* 20 (1954): 22–32; Mahdi Agha Husain, "Ibn Battuta, His Life and Work," *Indo-Iranica* 7 (1954): 6–13; G. H. Bousquet, "Ibn Battuta et les Institutions Musulmanes," *Studia Islamica* 24 (1966): 81–106; Driss Chraibi, *Succession ouverte* (Paris: Denoël, 1962); Driss Chraibi, *Le Passe Simple* (Paris: Denoël, 1954); Driss Chraibi, *The Simple Past,* trans. Hugh A. Harter (Washington, D.C.: Three Continents, 1990); Driss Chraibi, *Une Enquette Au Pays* (Paris: Editions du Seuil, 1981); Abdelhak Serhane, *Messaouda* (Paris: Editions du Seuil, 1983); Abdelhak Serhane, *Les Enfants des rues etroites* (Paris: Editions du Seuil, 1986); Abdelhak Serhane, *Le Soleil des Obscurs* (Paris: Editions du Seuil, 1992); Abdelhak Serhane, *L'amour circoncis* (Paris: Paris-Méditerranée, 2001); Mohammed Zefzaf, *Al-Mar'a wa al-warda* [The Woman and the Rose] (Beirut: Al-Dar-al-Muttahida li al-Nashr, 1970); Ahmed Sefrioui, *La Boîte a Merveilles* (Paris: Editions du Seuil, 1954); Ahmed Sefrioui, *Le jardin des sortilèges, ou, Le parfum des legends* (Paris: L'Harmattan, 1989); Ahmed Lemish, *Shkun Trez Lma …!?* (n.p., 1994); Liat Kozma, "Moroccan Women's Narrative of

Liberation: The Passive Revolution?" in James McDougall, ed., *Nation, Society and Culture in North Africa* (Portland, OR: Frank Cass, 2003); Leila Abouzeid, *Year of the Elephant: A Moroccan Woman's Journey towards Independence* (Austin: University of Texas Press, 1990); Leila Abouzeid, *Return to Childhood* (Austin: Center for Middle Eastern Studies, University of Texas, 1999); Leila Abouzeid, *The Last Chapter* (Cairo: American University Press, 2003); Amina El Bakouri, *Ra'ian Ya'tika Lmadih* (Rabat: Sais Midit, 2002); Touria Majdouline, *Leaves of Ash* (Rabat: Union of Moroccan Writers, 1990); Touria Majdouline, *The Weary* (Oujda, Morocco: Dar al Jusoor, 2000); Daniel A. Wagner, *Literacy, Culture, and Development: Becoming Literate in Morocco* (Cambridge: Cambridge University Press, 1993); *Annuaire Statique du Maroc* [Annual Statistics of Morocco] (Rabat: Ministry of Communication, 1999, 2000); Abdelmajid Hannoum, *Colonial Histories, Post-colonial Memories: The Legend of the Kahina, A North African Heroine* (Portsmouth, NH: Heinemann, 2001); Abdelmajid Hannoum, "Storytellers in Morocco," *Mediterraneans* (fall 1999): 189–194; Salah Moukhlis, "A History of Hopes Postponed: Women's Identity and the Postcolonial State in the Year of the Elephant: A Moroccan Woman's Journey Toward Independence," *Research in African Literatures* 34, no. 3 (fall 2003): 66–78; Ismail El-Outmani, "Prolegomena to the Study of the "Other" Moroccan Literature," *Research in African Literatures* 28, no. 3 (fall 1997): 110–122.

ART AND ARCHITECTURE/HOUSING

Wilhelmina Schripper, "The Verbal and the Visual in a Globalizing Context: African and European Connections as an Ongoing Process," *Research in African Literature* 31, no. 4 (2000): 139–154; Bogumil Jewsiewicki, *Cheri Samba: The Hybridity of Art* [*L' hybridité d' un art*] (Westmount, Quebec: Galerie Amrad African Art Publications, 1995); Richard F. Nyrop et al., *Area Handbook for Morocco* (Washington, D.C.: U.S. Government Printing Office, 1972); E. Gans-Ruedin, *The Connoisseur's Guide to Oriental Carpets,* trans. Valerie Howard (Rutland, VT: Charles E. Tuttle, 1971); Christine Mullen and Sarah Fez, eds., *Objects as Envoys: Cloth, Imagery, and Diplomacy in Madagascar* (Washington, D.C.: Smithsonian Institution, National Museum of African Art in association with University of Washington Press, 2002); Daniel J. Schroeter and Vivian B. Mann, eds., *Morocco: Jews and Art in a Muslim Land* (London: Merrell, 2000); James McDougall, ed., *Nation, Society and Culture in North Africa* (Portland, OR: Frank Cass, 2003); Katarzyna Pieprzak, "Citizens and Subjects in the Bank: Corporate Visions of Modern Art and Moroccan Identity," *Journal of North African Studies* 8, no. 1 (2003): 131–154; Nnamdi Elleh, *Architecture and Power in Africa* (Westport, CT: Praeger, 2002); Hsain Illahiane, "The Break-up of the Ksar: Changing Settlement Patterns and Environmental

Management in Southern Morocco," *Africa Today* 48, no. 1 (2001): 21–48; Roger Joseph and Terri Brint Joseph, *The Rose and the Thorn: Semiotic Structures in Morocco* (Tucson: University of Arizona Press, 1987); Dale F. Eickelman, "Is There an Islamic City? The Making of a Quarter in a Moroccan Town," *International Journal of Middle East Studies* 5 (1974): 274–294; Lawrence Rosen, "Muslim-Jewish Relations in a Moroccan City," *International Journal of Middle East Studies* 3 (1972): 435–449; Hans Seligo, *Morocco,* trans. G. A. Colville (Garden City, NY: Doubleday, 1966); Philippe Ploquin and Mohammed-Allal Sinaceur, *La Mosquée Hassan II* [The Hassan II Mosque], (Dremil-Lafage, France: Editions D. Briand, 1993); Ariella Amar, "Moroccan Synagogues: A Survey," *The Israeli Review of Arts and Letters* 106 (February 1999), 1–6; Daniel J. Schroeter, *The Sultan's Jew: Morocco and the Sephardi World* (Stanford, CA: Stanford University Press, 2002); Susan Gilson Miller, "Watering the Garden of Tangier: Colonial Contestations in a Moroccan City," in Susan Slyomovics, ed., *The Walled Arab City in Literature, Architecture and History: The Living Medina in the Maghrib* (Portland, OR: Frank Cass, 2001), 25–50.

CUISINE AND TRADITIONAL DRESS

Catherine Hanger, *World Food: Morocco* (Victoria, Australia: Lonely Planet, 2000); Paula Wolfert, *Couscous and Other Good Food from Morocco* (New York: Harper and Row, 1973); May Ellen Roach-Higgins, Joanne B. Eicher, and Kim K. P. Johnson, eds., *Dress and Identity* (New York: Fairchild, 1995); Hanna Goodman, *Jewish Cooking Around the World: Gourmet and Holiday Recipes* (Philadelphia: Jewish Society of America, 1969); Roger Joseph and Terri Brint Joseph, *The Rose and the Thorn: Semiotic Structures in Morocco* (Tucson: University of Arizona Press, 1987); Claudia Roden, *A Book of Middle Eastern Food* (New York: Alfred A. Knopf, 1972); C. R. Pennell, *Morocco since 1830: A History* (New York: New York University Press, 2000); Helen Mendes, *The African Heritage Cookbook* (New York: Macmillan, 1971); Harold D. Nelson, ed., *Morocco: A Country Study,* 4th ed. (Washington, D.C.: American University Press, 1978); Edmondo De Amicis, *Morocco: Its People and Places,* trans. Maria Hornor Lansdale (Philadelphia: Henry T. Coates, 1897); Susan Ossman, *Picturing Casablanca: Portraits of Power in a Modern City* (Berkeley: University of California Press, 1994); Susan Ossman, *Three Faces of Beauty: Casablanca, Paris, Cairo* (Durham, NC: Duke University Press, 2002). Daniel J. Schroeter and Joseph Chetrit, "The Transformation of Eassaoira (Mogador) in the Nineteenth and Twentieth Centuries," in Harvey E. Goldberg, ed., *Sephardi Middle Eastern Jewelries: History and Culture in the Modern Era* (Bloomington: Indiana University Press, 1996); Mounia Bennani-Chraibi, *Soumis et rebelles: les jeunes au Maroc* (Casablanca: Edition le Fennec,

1994), 89–100; Henry Munson, *Religion and Power in Morocco* (New Haven, CT: Yale University Press, 1993).

Gender Roles, Marriage, and Family

Sheila K. Webster, "Women, Sex, and Marriage in Moroccan Proverbs," *International Journal of Middle Eastern Studies* 14 (1982): 173–184; Roger Joseph and Terri Brint Joseph, *The Rose and the Thorn: Semiotic Structures in Morocco* (Tucson, University of Arizona Press, 1987); Ernest Gellner, *Saints of the Atlas* (London: Weidenfeld and Nicholson, 1969); David M. Hart, "The Tribe in Modern Morocco: Two Case studies," in Ernest Gellner and Charles Micaud, eds., *Arabs and Berbers: From Tribe to Nation in North Africa* (London: Duckworth, 1972); Robert Montagne, *The Berbers: Their Social and Political Organization,* trans. David Seddon (London: Frank Cass, 1973); Harold D. Nelson, ed., *Morocco: A Country Study* (Washington, D.C.: American University Press, 1978); Carolyn Fluehr-Lobban, *Islamic Societies in Practice,* 2nd ed. (Gainesville: University of Florida Press, 2004); Vanessa Maher, *Women and Property in Morocco* (Cambridge: Cambridge University Press, 1974); Robert Elbaz, "Toward a Comprehensive Socio-Cultural Theory of the Jewish Life-World in Morocco: The Jewish Traditional Marriage in Morocco," *Extenza: International Journal of Francophone Studies* 7, no. 1 (June 2004): 95–101; M. E. Combs-Schilling, *Sacred Performances: Islam, Sexuality, and Sacrifice* (New York: Columbia University Press, 1989); Douglas A. Davis and Susan Schaefer Davis, "Sexual Values in a Moroccan Town," in W. J. Lonner and R. S. Malpass, eds., *Psychology and Culture* (Needham Heights, MA: Allyn and Bacon, 1993); Rachel Simon, "Between the Family and the Outside World: Jewish Girls in the Modern Middle East and North Africa," *Jewish Social Studies* 7, no. 1 (2000): 81–108; Amal Rassam, "Women and Domestic Power in Morocco," *International Journal of Middle Eastern Studies* 12 (1980): 171–183; Hillary Mayell, "Thousands of Women Killed for Family 'Honor,'" *National Geography News,* 12 February 2002, 1–2; International Food and Agricultural Development, *Survival, Change and Decision-Making in Rural Households: Three Village Case Studies from Eastern Morocco* (Rome: IFAD, 1997); Fatima Mernissi, *Doing Daily Battles: Interviews with Moroccan Women,* trans. Mary Jo Lakeland (New Brunswick, NJ: Rutgers University Press, 1989); Fatima Agnaou, *Gender, Literacy, and Empowerment in Morocco* (New York: Routledge, 2004); Eltigani E. Eltigani, "Changes in Family-Building Patterns in Egypt and Morocco: A Comparative Analysis," *International Family Planning Perspectives* 26, no. 2 (June 2003): 73–78; Jamila Bargach, *Orphans of Islam: Family, Abandonment, and Secret Adoption in Morocco* (Lanham, MD: Rowman and Littlefield, 2002).

SOCIAL CUSTOMS AND LIFESTYLE

Roger Joseph Jr., *Rituals and Relatives: A Study of Social Uses of Wealth in Morocco* (Ann Arbor, MI: University Microfilms International, 1979); Carolyn Fluehr-Lobban, *Islamic Societies in Practice,* 2nd ed. (Gainesville: University Press of Florida, 2004); Dale F. Eickelman, *Moroccan Islam: Tradition and Society in a Pilgrimage Center* (Austin: University of Texas Press, 1976); E. W. Bovill, *The Golden Trade of the Moors* (Oxford: Oxford University Press, 1968); Hamadi Gueroum, "History of Moroccan Cinema," excerpts from the program of the 24th Festival of the 3 Continents, Nantes, France, November 2002; Kevin Dwyer, *Beyond Casablanca: M. A. Tazi, Moroccan Cinema, and Third World Filmmaking* (Bloomington: Indiana University Press, 2004); Daniel A. Wagner, *Literacy, Culture, and Development: Becoming Literate in Morocco* (New York: Cambridge University Press, 1993); 1998; C. R. Pennell, *Morocco since 1830: A History* (New York: New York University Press, 2000).

MUSIC AND DANCE

For an interesting introduction to African traditional music, see W. Komla Amoaku, "Towards a Definition of Traditional African Music: A Look at the Ewe of Ghana," in Irene V. Jackson, ed., *More Than Drumming* (Westport, CT: Greenwood, 1985). Valérie K. Orlando, "From Rap to Rai in the Mixing Bowl: Beur Hip-Hop Culture and Banlieue Cinema in Urban France," *Journal of Popular Culture* 36, no. 3 (winter 2003): 395–415. For specific studies on Moroccan music, see the Paul Bowles Moroccan Music Collection AFC 1960/001, comp. Michelle Forner (Washington, D.C.: Library of Congress, 1994); Josef Pacholczyk, review: "The Pan-Islamic Tradition: Music of Morocco by Philip Schuyler," *Ethnomusicology* 19, 1 (January, 1973), 154–55; Harold D. Nelson, ed., *Morocco: A Country Study,* 4th ed. (Washington, D.C.: American University Press, 1978); Eugene Fodor and William Curtis, *Fodor's Morocco 1973* (New York: David McKay, 1973); Deborah A. Kapchan, "Moroccan Female Performers Defining the Social Body," *Journal of American Folklore* 107, no. 423 (winter 1994): 82–105; Deborah A. Kapchan, *Gender on the Market: The Revoicing of Tradition in Beni Mellal, Morocco* (Philadelphia: University of Pennsylvania Press, 1996); Lila Abu-Lughod, *Veiled Sentiments: Honor and Poetry in a Bedouin Society* (Berkeley: University of California Press, 1986); Abdelkabir Khatibi, *La Memoire Tatouee* (Paris: Editions Denoël, 1971); Bernard Lortat-Jacob, *Musique et Fetes du Haut-Atlas* [Music and Festivals of the High Atlas] (Paris: Mouton, 1980); David Prescott Barrows, *Berbers and Blacks: Impressions of Morocco, Timbuktu, and the Western Sudan* (Westport, CT: Negro Universities Press, 1987).

Index

About the Author

RAPHAEL CHIJIOKE NJOKU is Assistant Professor of African History at the University of Louisville, Kentucky, and an adjunct at Indiana University Southeast.